AF600518

THE CATHOLIC UNIVERSITY OF AMERICA
CANON LAW STUDIES
No. 219

The Free Conferral of Offices

A HISTORICAL SYNOPSIS AND COMMENTARY

BY

JOSEPH LEROY MANNING, J. C. L.
Priest of the Archdiocese of San Antonio

A DISSERTATION

Submitted to the Faculty of the School of Canon Law of the Catholic University of America in Partial Fulfillment of the Requirements for the Degree of Doctor of Canon Law

THE CATHOLIC UNIVERSITY OF AMERICA PRESS, Inc.
WASHINGTON, D. C.
1945

NIHIL OBSTAT:

EDUARDUS ROELKER, S.T.D., J.C.D.,

Censor Deputatus.

Washingtonii, D. C., die 30 *aprilis,* 1945.

IMPRIMATUR:

†ROBERTUS E. LUCEY, D.D.,

Archiepiscopus Sancti Antonii.

Sancti Antonii, 10 *maii,* 1945.

Printed by
Schneider Printing Company
San Antonio, Texas

To

MY FATHER AND MOTHER

TABLE OF CONTENTS

TABLE OF CONTENTS

FOREWORD

An ecclesiastical office is a function established by divine or ecclesiastical authority, permanent in character, to be conferred in the form and under the conditions prescribed by the sacred canons, and implying some participation in ecclesiastical power either of orders or of jurisdiction. Each office has its specific purpose. Each office carries with it definite obligations and is endowed with specific powers. But all ecclesiastical offices have this in common that they are the seats of jurisdiction and administration whence radiates that power which Christ gave to His Church for ruling and governing men toward the attainment of perfect happiness.

When the incumbent of an office exercises fully and judiciously the powers of his office to fulfill the obligations of the office, then and then only is the purpose of the office adequately accomplished. Holy Mother Church, therefore, has been solicitous throughout the centuries that all of her offices have worthy and capable incumbents. It is to be expected that this solicitude would beget legislation, both general and particular, to oppose those forces and influences which might seek to undermine her authority over her offices or to place in them the unworthy or incompetent.

This general legislation on the conferral of offices, general in the sense that it pertains to all offices, is contained in the Code of Canon Law in the first chapter of title IV in the second book. Within this chapter are the norms which govern all types of canonical assignments of office and also those which govern the three specific types, namely, free conferral (*libera collatio*), election (*electio*), and postulation (*postulatio*). It is the general norms of free conferral, canons 152-159, which constitute the subject of this work.

This treatise is divided into two parts. The first part reflects an attempt to trace in pre-Code legislation the enactments which were to serve as the foundations of the present laws. By the eleventh century the vast majority of ecclesiastical offices had been endowed with sources of revenue and had become known as benefices. It was not until recent centuries that these endowments began their rapid disappearance. Consequently the reader will look in vain in the *Corpus Iuris Canonici* or even in subsequent legislation for laws on offices as distinct from benefices. The historical analysis, therefore, will have as its purpose to ascertain whether the primary object of the pertinent enactments was to deal with offices in themselves or with the temporalities conjoined to them.

The second part presents a canonical commentary in which an attempt has been made to indicate the law of the Code on free conferral, and along with it to offer an interpretation of this law.

The writer takes this occasion to acknowledge most sincerely his gratitude to the Most Reverend Robert E. Lucey, Archbishop of San Antonio, for the opportunity of further studies in Canon Law. Appreciation is also acknowledged to the Most Reverend Sidney M. Metzger, Bishop of El Paso, and to the Most Reverend Laurence J. FitzSimon, Bishop of Amarillo, for the interest they have shown, and to the Rt. Rev. Patrick J. Geehan, Vicar General of the Archdiocese of San Antonio, for his many kindnesses and encouragement. Finally, a debt of gratitude is due to the Faculty of the School of Canon Law of the Catholic University of America for assistance in the preparation of this study.

HISTORICAL SYNOPSIS

CHAPTER I

The Law Prior To The Council of Trent

Prior to the Council of Trent offices without endowments for their incumbents were practically non-existent, and for this reason the *Corpus Iuris Canonici* and the Decretals speak solely of benefices. In pre-Code as in post-Code law, however, the office is the essential foundation of the benefice.[1]

For instance, prior to the Code there were dignities (*dignitates*), such as the Archdiaconate in cathedral and collegiate chapters, which were canonries to which the right of precedence and the power of jurisdiction in the external forum were attached;[2] there were simple canonries to which the right of precedence was attached without any power of jurisdiction, as, for example, the ranking functionaries (*primicerii*),[3] and, finally, there were the simple offices or simple canonries which carried with them neither any right of precedence nor any power of jurisdiction, but merely the right to administer certain ecclesiastical goods, as, for example, the offices of sacristans (*sacristae*)[4] and treasurers (*thesaurarii*).[5]

Ioannes Andreae (1272-1348) reserved the term "office" for those simple canonries which had annexed to them neither precedence nor jurisdiction,[6] but the term was more frequently used to designate any

---

[1] Wernz, *Ius Decretalium ad usum Praelectionum in Scholis Textus Iuris Canonici, sive Iuris Decretalium* (3. ed., 6 vols., Prati, 1915), II, n. 767 (hereafter cited as *Ius Decretalium*); Pistocchi, *De Re Beneficiali* (Taurini; Marietti, 1928), p. 43; Cappello, *Summa Iuris Canonici* (3 vols., Vol. 1, 3 ed., 1938; Vol. II, 3. ed., 1939; Vol. III, 1936; Romae: Apud Aedes Universitatis Gregorianae), II, n. 470.

[2] Cf. c. 54, X, *de electione et electi potestate,* I, 6.

[3] Cf. c. un., X, *de officio rimicerii,* I, 25.

[4] Cf. c. un., X, *de officio sacristae,* 1, 26.

[5] Cf. c. 1, X, *de officio custodis,* I, 27.

[6] " . . . tamen propie ista tria, dignitas, personatus, et officium differunt: nam dignitatem proprie dicitur quis habere qui habet administrationem, et cum hoc habet iurisdictionem . . . sed personatus dicitur is habere qui in ecclesia habet aliquam praeeminentiam, non tamen habet iurisdictionem . . . ., officium vero dicitur quis habere qui sine iurisdictione et sine praeeminentia habet administrationem rerum ecclesiasticarum."—*Glossa* ad c. 1, *de consuetudine,* I, 4, in VI°, in principio.

ecclesiastical function.[7] Because of the endowments which all offices possessed, the term "benefice" will be used in this historical synopsis as synonymous with office, unless it be explicitly stated otherwise.

ARTICLE I

FREE CONFERRAL

In his memorable *Regulae Iuris* Boniface VIII (1294-1303) gave first place to the principle that an ecclesiastical benefice cannot be obtained licitly without canonical institution.[8] Cardinal Hostiensis (*Henricus de Segusio,* who died in 1271), in his monumental work on the decretals, stated that by institution (*institutio*) was meant nothing more or less than the act by which a cleric was given charge of a benefice by one who possessed the legitimate authority to designate him; through it there was accorded the right to take canonical possession.[9] Ioannes Andreae taught that institution (*institutio*) implied a threefold act, namely, the giving of title to the office, the commission to care for souls (which of course was absent if the care of souls was not annexed to the office), and the introduction into possession.[10] This threefold act followed upon the designation by election, presentation, or nomination, of the person who was to obtain the office. This same author reserved the term *collatio* for that specific type of conferral wherein one and the same superior had the unrestricted right of nominating the candidate, of giving him title, and of committing to him the care of souls.[11]

---

[7] Cf. c. 8. X, *de constitutionibus,* I, 2; Wernz, *Ius Decretalium,* II, n. 240, § 2.

[8] Reg. 1, R. J., in VI°.

[9] *Commentaria in Quinquc Decretalium Libros* (5 vols. in 3, ed. Venetiis, 1581), tit. *de officio vicarii,* c. *ad haec* (I, 28, 3), v. *instituit.*

[10] "Dicendum quod triplex est institutio: quaedam est institutio tituli collativa: alia est institution auctorizabilis quo ad commissionem curae animarum: alia est institutio realis et actualis, quae vocatur investitura vel inductio in possessionem realem et corporalem."—*Glossa* ad reg. 1, R. J. in VI°, s. v. *beneficium.*

[11] " . . . collatio autem dictur quae fit de beneficio non Patronato; quod spectat ad episcopum pleno iure sine praesentatione patroni."—*Glossa* ad reg. 1, R. J. in VI°, s. v. *beneficium.*

ARTICLE II. THE ORDINARY COLLATOR

The attacks directed against the right of the Supreme Pontiff to the and full conferral of all ecclesiastical offices in the Church, and of the bishop to those within his jurisdiction, have always taken the form of restriction of its exercise rather than of theological or philosophical issues. As outstanding examples of these attacks there were the practices, on the part of the Byzantine emperors, of instituting and deposing bishops, and the abuses consequent on the proprietary church, which led to the great investiture contest of the eleventh and twelfth centuries. As a direct result of this contest Gratian incorporated in his *Concordia Discordantium Canonum* various texts derived from the councils and from the letters of the popes which were directed toward the protection and vindication of the right of the hierarchy over ecclesiastical offices and the free exercise of that right. It may be noted, however, that in these texts there is no explicit mention of the right of the Supreme Pontiff, the reason for this being that the popes did not commence the practice of conferring offices in the dioceses of other bishops until the year 1137,[12] and hence the seldom invoked exercise of their right was comparatively free from attack.

For example, Gratian embodied in his work canon 17 of the first Council of Orleans (511), which declared that all churches which had been constructed in various places, as well as those yet to be built, pertained to the jurisdiction of the bishop in whose territory they were situated,[13] an excerpt from a letter of Pope Leo IV (847-855) written in the year 849 to the bishops of Britain insisting that every parish be provided for, be governed and guarded, by the bishop,[14] and a canon of the I General Council of the Lateran (1123), warning archdeacons and archpriests that they were not to confer offices without the con-

---

12 Hinschius, *System des katholischen Kirchenrechts* (4 vols., Berlin, 1869-1888), III, 114; Barraclough, *Papal Provisions* (Oxford: Basil Blackwell, 1935), p. 4.

13 C. 10, C. XVI, q. 7; *Monumenta Germaniae Historica, Legum Sectio III, Concilia aevi Merovingici* (ed. Fridericus Maasen, Hannoveriae, 1893), I, 6.

14 C. 4, C. X, q. 1; Jaffé, *Regesta Pontificum Romanorum ab Condita Ecclesiae ad annum post Christum natum MCXCVIII* (2 ed. correcta et aucta [*ab condita Ecclesiae ad annum DXC* ed. Kaltenbrunner; *ab anno DXC ad annum DCCCLXXXII*, ed. Ewald; *ab anno DCCCXLXXII ad annum MCXCVIII*, ed. Loewenfeld,] 2 vols. in 1, Lipsiae, 1885-1888), JE, n. 2599.

sent of the bishop.[15] Gratian himself in one of his rubrics stated that in general both churches and ecclesiastical things pertain to the authority of the bishop.[16]

The right of the Supreme Pontiff to the free and full conferral of all offices in the church, and of the bishop to the conferral of those which his jurisdiction, finds more concrete expression in the Decretals, even though it was still to a great extent restricted in its exercise by the acquired rights of others. These rights of election,[17] presentation,[18] patronage,[19] postulation,[20] reservation,[21] and consent,[22] were found in the hands of individual or moral persons as acquired by law, privilege, custom, or prescription. Many of them were remnants of the Germanic law and the proprietary church era, extant by reason of the compromise in the Concordat of Worms (1122) and the corresponding concordats with France and England. More definite and particular leglation, however, was needed for putting into exercise those rights which these concordats had vindicated, which legislation was enacted particularly by Alexander III (1159-1181).

In a decretal to the Archbishop of Canterbury and his suffragans this pope declared the acquisition of benefices without the consent of the bishop to be a custom reprehensible and illegal, which had to be stamped out.[23] He branded the conferral of churches by laymen as null and void,[24] and insisted that the authority of the bishop was necessary for the acquisition of a benefice.[25] In the III General Council (1179) he explicitly extended to religious his injunction against the receiving of churches from the laity, and warned them to avoid instituting priests in, or removing them from, churches which had not been entrusted to them *pleno iure*.[26]

---

[15] C. 11, C. XVI, q. 7; Mansi, *Sacrorum Conciliorum Nova et Amplissima Collectio* (53 vols. in 60, Parisiis, Arnhem, Lipsiae, 1901-1927), XXI, 282.

[16] Dictum in principio, C. XVI, q. 7.

[17] Cf. c. 7, X, *de electione et electi potestate*, I, 6.

[18] Cf. c. 4, *de clericis non residentibus in ecclesia vel praebenda*, III, 4.

[19] Cf. tit. 38, X, *de iure patronatus*, III.

[20] Cf. tit. 5, X, *de postulatione praelatorum*, I.

[21] Cf. c. 2, *de praebendis et dignitatibus*, III, 4, in VI°.

[22] Cf. c. 4, X, *de his quae fiunt a praelato sine consensu capituli*, III, 10.

[23] C. 3, X, *de institutionibus*, III, 7; JL, n. 13817.

[24] C. 5, X, *de iure patronatus*, III, 38; JL, n. 14346; Mansi, XXII, 336.

[25] C. 4, X, *de iure patronatus*, III, 38; Mansi, XXII, 227.

[26] C. 9—Mansi, XXII, 222; c. 3, X, *de privilegiis et excessibus privilegiatorum*, V, 33.

Innocent III (1198-1216) in the first year of his pontificate prefaced one of his letters of papal provision with the notice that he could effect the provision in virtue of the fullness of the power given to him.[27] He added little to the law, merely repeating the principles already set forth, but a decretal issued by him on August 9, 1206, is worthy of note in that it upholds the claim of a bishop to the *intentio fundata* for the conferring of all vacant churches in his diocese.[28] This appears to be the first use of this phrase in this regard.

Finally, in his decree *Licet Ecclesiarum,* issued on August 27, 1265, Clement IV (1265-1268) stated that the plenary disposition of all churches, personable rankings, dignities, and benefices, belongs to the Roman Pontiff.[29] Ioannes Andreae, however, made mention of even this power as being restricted in its exercise by any extant right of presentation.[30]

The Supreme Pontiff, therefore, was recognized as having in principle the full and free disposition of all ecclesiastical offices, and similarly the bishop was recognized as the ordinary collator of the offices within his jurisdiction.

ARTICLE III. THE EXTRAORDINARY COLLATOR

The free and full conferral of offices could pass from the hands off the ordinary collator in three ways, namely, 1) by privilege, custom, or prescription; 2) by papal reservation; and 3) by means of other positive legislation. The first of these means has been touched on in the preceding articles, and in the present work it needs to receive but a passing notice since its discussion belongs to other specialized fields. The second has been treated by Haydt in his dissertation Reserved Benefices.[31]

The third way in which the power of conferral could pass from the hands of the ordinary collator, prescinding from concordats, had as the reason for its existence the possibility of neglect or failure on the part of the ordinary collator in fulfilling his office. Prior to the III General Lateran Council (1179) there existed few instances of the

---

27 Potthast, *Regesta Pontificum Romanorum inde ab anno post Christum natum MCXCVIII ad annum MCCCIV* (2 vols., Berolini, 1874-1875), n. 83.

28 C. 6, X, *de exceptionibus,* II, 25; Potthast, n. 3791.

29 C. 2, *de praebendis et dignitatibus,* III, 4, in VI°; Potthast, n. 19326.

30 *Glossa* ad c. 2, *de praebendis et dignitatibus,* III, 4, in VI°, s. v. *Collatio.*

31 The Catholic University of America Canon Law Studies, n. 161 (Washington, D.C.: The Catholic University of America Press, 1942).

ius devolutivum. In the year 601 St. Gregory the Great wrote to the subdeacon Antemius that, in the event that the bishop neglected to appoint a *vicedominus* and a *major domus,* the clergy should assemble and elect worthy persons for these offices.[32] The length of time to be allowed the bishop for making these appointments received no mention in this nor in the next instance of such legislation, namely, canon 11 of the II General Council of Nicea (787)[33] which prescribed that metropolitans were to supply any defect on the part of their suffragans in appointing the procurator required by the Council of Chalcedon (451)[34] and that suffragans were to supply any defect in this matter on the part of their metropolitans.

A limit of three months beyond which a church was not to continue vacant had been set by St. Gregory in 597 in a letter to the Bishop of Ravenna.[35] This prescription was repeated in the II General Lateran Council (1139).[36] But in neither instance was mention made that, in case of default, the power to fill the office should pass to another collator.

The first general legislation, the conciliar decree *Nulla ecclesiastica,* was enacted in the III General Lateran Council under Alexander III. A period of six months was allowed within which the collator was to confer a vacant benefice or office upon a worthy incumbent. Upon the lapse of the six months the power of conferral passed from the hands of the bishop to the chapter, or from the chapter to the bishop. If both the bishop and the chapter failed to fulfill their duty, the power of conferral passed to the metropolitan.[37] This law remained the *ius devolutivum* until the promulgation of the Code.

It is worthy of note that this law made provision for the passing of the power from a superior to an inferior, namely, from the bishop to the chapter. Nevertheless Bernard of Parma (†1266), the author of the ordinary gloss to the Decretals of Gregory IX, could remark that the opposite was the ordinary procedure.[38]

It remained for Innocent III to give the authentic interpretation of

---

32 C. 2, D. LXXXIX; JE, n. 1845.

33 Mansi, XIII, 429; C. 3, C. IX, q. 3.

34 C. 26—Mansi, VII, 399; C. 21, C. XVI, q. 7.

35 C. 11, D. L; JE, n. 1485.

36 C. 28—Mansi, XXI, 533.

37 C. 8—Mansi, XXII, 222; c. 2, X, *de concessione praebendae et ecclesiae non vacantis,* III, 8.

38 *Glossa* ad. c. 7, X, *deelectione et electi potestate,* I, 6, s. v. *capitulum.*

this law, particularly in clarifying what allotment of time was granted by the law for the conferral of the vacant office. He declared that the prescribed time was to be computed, not from the date of the vacancy of the office, but from the date of the notice thereof received by him to whom the power of conferral pertained. He further explained that as part of the six months which were allotted by the conciliar statute, *Nulla ecclesiastica,* there was not to be computed the time during which the collator was under suspension, nor the time needed for his journey to Rome, for his stay there, and for his return.[39] He likewise decreed that, once the time had elapsed, any assignment of office thereafter effected by him to whom the power of conferral had previously pertained was void of all juridical effect.[40] Finally, he provided legislation on the point which had been left unconsidered by the Lateran Council, namely, that should the metropolitan be negligent in conferring the offices within his own jurisdiction, or in fulfilling his duty as an extraordinary collator, the right of appointment would then, in the absence of any intermediate superior, revert to the Supreme Pontiff.[41] The latter, although he had ordinary and plenary jurisdiction over all offices, thus became the extraordinary collator with reference to the office in question.

According to Alexander III the *ius devolutivum* also became effective immediately when the ordinary collator in bad faith had conferred an office on one by law disqualified for receiving it.[42] Innocent III added that the same rule held when the office was given to an unworthy candidate,[43] but Boniface VIII decreed that, at least in so far as elections were concerned, if the body of electors had acted in good faith in electing an unworthy candidate, an additional six months was granted for the holding of another election.[44]

To which offices did the mandatory exercise of this *ius devolutivum* apply? In 1208 Innocent III explained in one of his decretals that it

---

39 C. 5, X, *de concessione praebendae et ecclesiae non vacantis,* III, 8; Potthast, n. 678.

40 C. 5, X, *de supplenda negligentia praelatorum,* I, 10; Potthast, n. 4110.

41 C. 3, X, *de supplenda negligentia praelatorum,* I, 10; Potthast, n. 5035.

42 C. 7, X, *de electione et electi potestate,* I, 6; Mansi, XXII, 219.

43 C. 11, X, *de excessibus praelatorum et subditorum,* V, 31; Potthast, n. 3662.

44 C. 26, *de electione et electi potestate,* I, 6, in VI°.

was the custom not to extend it to bishoprics and archbishoprics.[45] The reason for this was that these offices had already become the objects of special legislation as early as the year 597, when St. Gregory in a letter to the Bishop of Ravenna decreed that they be filled within three months of their vacancy.[46] The import of this law was confirmed in the II General Lateran Council,[47] and thereafter remained in force concurrently with the later conciliar decree *Nulla ecclelsiastica.*[48]

This same legislation was re-enacted in the IV General Lateran Council (1215), wherein it was also decreed that the ordinary collator had but three months in which to confer cathedral and monastic churches.[49] So far as the monastic church was concerned, this law applied only to the office of the abbot. But for the bishop and the abbot there was granted an additional period of three months, during which the bishop was to receive the episcopal consecration and the abbot the abbatial blessing.[50]

ARTICLE IV. INCOMPATABILITY OF OFFICES

It can be affirmed without hesitation that as much space, both in Gratian and in the Decretals, has been given to legislation regarding the matter of incompatible offices as to legislation on any other individual point in law. It was, moreover, a major point and a point of major importance to the glossators, their contemporaries, and to the authors of succeeding centuries. The evolution of the law is clear enough, but both the principles and the application furnished material for discussion and controversy.

For the purpose of a clearer understanding and a safer interpretation of the law as it binds in the present, it has been deemed advisable to

---

45 C. 12, X, *de concessione praebendae et ecclesiae non vacantis,* III, 8; Potthast, n. 3449.

46 C. 11, D. L; JE, n. 1485.

47 Mansi, XXI, 533; C. 35, D. LXIII.

48 *Glossa* ad. c. 12, X, *de concessione praebendae et ecclesiae non vacantis,* III, 8, s. v. *extendi.*

49 " . . . statuimus ut ultra tres menses cathedralis vel regularis ecclesia praelato non vacet, . . . ac ipsa elegendi potestas ad eum qui proximo praeesse dignoscitur devolvatur."—C. 41, X, *de electione et electi potestate,* I, 6; Mansi, XXII, 1011.

50 Cf. Hostiensis, *Commentaria,* tit. *de electione et electi potestate,* c. *Ne pro defctu* (I, 6, 41), n. 2.

place the analysis of the pre-Code prohibitions against a multiplicity of offices in juxta position to the canonical commentary on the same point.

ARTICLE V. ORDER REQUISITE FOR THE CARE OF SOULS

In the early centuries when the population of the Christian world was centered in and around the towns and cities, it was comparatively easy for the bishops, who were in every city and who alone were officially charged with the care of souls, to exercise this care with the assistance of a few priests and a number of clerics. But as the population spread and chapels were erected for the people in the rural districts and smaller towns, it became evident that, while the clerics who were sent to these churches could be enabled to care for souls in so far as jurisdiction was concerned, they could not, in view of their lack of priestly orders, effectively meet all the serious dangers which beset the eternal salvation of the souls entrusted to their care. Hence, as early as the time of the Council of Elvira (305), serious legislative consideration was given to this matter even though the legislation did not accord full recognition to the fact that in the priesthood alone was contained the power of orders which sufficed for the effective administration of this charge.[51] An indirect approach to the problem was made through subsequent legislation on the age requisite for the reception of orders and for incumbency in an office to which was attached the care of souls.

The law prior to and at the time of Gratian demanded that a cleric be thirty years of age for ordination to the priesthood.[52] Rufinus († ca. 1190), however, stated that the age of twenty-five was sufficient in a case of necessity.[53] There was no direct change in this law in the Decretals, but, as will be shown presently, some commentators held that it was superseded indirectly.

In his collection of the Gregorian Decretals St. Raymond of Penafort (1175-1275) embodied a canon of the Council of Poitiers (1078), which required that if abbots, deans, and prelates were not priests

---

51 Cf. c. 77—Mansi, II, 18.

52 Council of Neocaesarea (314), c. 11—Mansi, II, 541; c. 4, D. LXXVIII; Bonifacius I (418-422), *Si quis triginta*—JK, n. † 356; Council of Agde (506), c. 17—Mansi, VIII, 327; c. 6, D. LXXVIII.

53 *Die Summa des Magister Rufinus,* ad D. LXXVIII, s. v. *qua vero aetate.*

they were to receive ordination to the priesthood.[54] More pertinent legislation, however, is to be found in the decretals of Alexander III and in a canon of the III General Lateran Council (1179). In writing to the Archbishop of Canterbury and his suffragans, Alexander, in his decretal *Indecorem* forbade the conferring of any church upon those who were under fourteen years of age,[55] and in a later decretal, the *Praeterea licet,* demanded that those who had received parochial churches had to become priests within a short time if they wished to hold them.[56] But these decretals can be fully understood only in conjunction with the conciliar statute *Cum in cunctis* of the III General Lateran Council, which decreed that an office which had the care of souls attached to it could not be given to one who had not reached his twenty-fifth year of age, and that, if it was given to one who was not a priest, then the recipient of the office had to receive ordination to the priesthood within the time allowed, or else be deprived of the office.[57] Thus, in one decretal it was forbidden to give any church to a cleric who was under fourteen years of age, and in another decretal, it was forbidden to give an office invested with the care of souls to one under twenty-five years of age. Even so, Bernard of Parma [58] and Hostiensis [59] stated that while a bishop could not dispense in favor of one under fourteen years of age, he could do so in favor of one who was between the age of fourteen and the age of twenty-five. When such a dispensation was granted, the care of souls was to be exercised by a priest until the recipient became of age for ordination.

Bernard of Parma considered the *breve tempus* mentioned in the decretal *Praeterea licet* as implying a period of four months,[60] that is, the recipient of the parochial office had to receive priestly ordination

---

[54] C. 7—Mansi, XX, 498; c. 1, X, *de aetate et qualitate et ordine praeficiendorum,* I, 14.

[55] C. 3, X, *de aetate et qualitate et ordine praeficiendorum,* I, 14; JL, n. 13820.

[56] C. 5, X, *de aetate et qualitate et ordine praeficiendorum,* I, 14; JL, n. 14219.

[57] C. 3—Mansi, XXII, 218; c. 7, X, *de electione et electi potestate,* I, 6.

[58] *Glossa* ad c, X, *de aetate et qualitate et ordine praeficiendorum,* I, 14, s. v. *infra XIIII annum.*

[59] *Commentaria,* tit. *de electione et electi potestate,* c. *Cum in cunctis,* (I, 6, 7), n. 10.

[60] *Glossa* ad c. 5, X, *de aetate et qualitate et ordine praeficiendorum,* I, 14, s. v. *breve tempus.*

on one of the Ember Days following his appointment.[61] This however, was definitely settled by Gregory X in the II General Council of Lyons (1274) wherein a year was indicated as the time within which the recipient was to receive ordination to the priesthood.[62]

Bernard was also of the opinion that, if a cleric at the age of twenty-five received a parochial church, or office to which was attached the care of souls, he needed no dispensation from the law which required that he be thirty years of age to become ordained to the priesthood.[63] But Hostiensis, while he admitted that custom interpreted these canons as setting the age of ordination to the priesthood at twenty-five years, considered the customary practice as an abuse.[64]

Finally, a decretal of Alexander III and two of Boniface VIII gave rise to a controversy as to the exact status which at the time of his appointment was demanded of the recipient of an office invested with the care of souls. In his decretal *Praeterea licet* Alexander III declared that one who received a parochial church had to be at least a subdeacon, although one in minor orders could receive such an office in virtue of a dispensation.[65]

Boniface VIII, however, decreed that those who had received apostolic letters which authorized the reception of a benefice were not to be barred from entering upon the possession of the benefice in view of any lack of orders on their part, even though the benefice was one which was invested with the care of souls.[66] He issued a similar decretal in regard to those who had been rightfully presented for institution in a parochial benefice, provided only that they could be promoted to orders within the time limit set by law.[67] The controversy, which continued until the promulgation of the Code of Canon Law, centered about the question whether these decretals of Boniface VIII constituted exceptions to the law of Alexander III, or whether they abrogated the earlier law.[68]

---

61 Cf. c. 1, 2, 3, X, *de temporibus ordinationum et qualitate ordinandorum,* I, 11.

62 C. 14, *de electione et electi potestate,* I, 6, in VI°.

63 *Glossa* ad c. 7, X, *de electione et electi potestate,* I, 6, s. v. *attigerit.*

64 *Commentaria,* tit. *de electione et electi potestate,* c. *Cum in cunctis,* (I, 6, 7), nn. 32-33.

65 C. 5, X, *de aetate et qualitate et ordine praeficiendorum,* I 14; JL, n. 14219.

66 C. 8, *de praebendis et dignitatibus,* III, 4, in VI°.

67 C. 2, *de institutionibus,* III, 6, in VI°; Potthast n. 24311.

ARTICLE VI. THE RESCRIPT

The conferral of an office in the Church, to be effective, had to be intimated to the one who was to receive the office, either in the form of an answer to a request or in the form of a rescript given *motu proprio* by the one who exercised the power of conferral. In this matter the law of the Decretals placed two particular conditions as necessary for validity, namely, that in the petition there be no subreption in regard to other benefices possessed, and that the rescript, at least when it was obtained from the Holy See, be in writing.

Rescripts in the matter of the conferral or of the reception of ecclesiastical offices were regulated in accordance with the general law on rescripts.[69] Moreover, by direct legislation a rescript for the reception of a benefice granted *ad preces* was invalid if in the petition the petitioner himself concealed the fact of his possession of another benefice. In accord with the law as it first appeared under Alexander III in the III General Lateran Council, the petitioner had to make mention of the already possessed benefice only if its revenues and income were sufficient for his sustenance.[70] Innocent III in 1214 made it clear that this law comprised within its scope also the perpetual vicarages which provided a sufficient sustenance for the incumbent.[71] Among the decretalists Bernard of Parma advised that in the petition mention be made even of a benefice whose income was not sufficient, and he warned that any false statement about such benefices certainly invalidated the grant contained in the rescript.[72]

Clement V distinguished between grants made by the Holy See and its legates, and grants made by inferior collators. He decreed that subreption in the petition did not of itself vitiate a rescript when it was issued by a metropolitan, a bishop, or an inferior.[73] But it might occur

---

[68] Ioannes Andreae: "Olim de iure communi tales ad talia beneficia non poterant assumi: hodie dicunt quidam indistincte quod possunt. Sed non sum ausus corrigere decretales."—*Glossa* ad c. 8, *de praebendis et dignitatibus*, III, 4, in VI°, s. v. *providere.*

[69] *Glossa* ad c. 42, X, *de rescriptis*, I 3, s. v. *de hac mentione.*

[70] C. 6, X, *de praebendis et dignitatibus*, III, 5.

[71] C. 27, X, *de rescriptis*, I, 3; Potthast, N. 4873.

[72] Glossa ad c. 17, X, *de rescriptis*, I, 3, s. v. *de praebenda.*

[73] C. 2, *de officio iudicis ordinarii*, I, 9, in Clem.

that by the grant contained in the rescript the recipient was to obtain a benefice incompatible with one he already had, in which case it was disputed whether the cleric lost the first benefice, or whether the rescript was invalid.

It is to be noted, first of all, that there was a general acceptance of the principle which insisted that the rescript was invalid if the petitioner himself was the culpable cause of the subreption in the petition for the benefice.[74] Secondly, the possession of a benefice did not invalidate the grant of a rescript when it was issued *motu proprio*. The reason for this was that such a rescript, even though a petition had been made, did not depend on the petition for any motivating cause.[75] But was a rescript issued *motu proprio* valid when thereby one gained possession of incompatible offices? Was a dispensation implied even when the Supreme Pontiff was ignorant of its necessity?

Panormitanus (1385-1453, following the opinion of Ioannes Andreae, held that the intention of the Pontiff had to be clear in such a case; otherwise the rescript was invalid.[76] But it is rather difficult to see how he could hold this opinion in the face of a decree of Clement V which declared that the grant of a papal rescript which conferred a benefice was valid regardless of the number or kind of benefice, offices, or dignities the recipient already possessed, even though no mention of these was made in the rescript.[77] The fact that Panormitanus cited Ioannes Andreae in support of his doctrine has little weight, for when Ioannes Andreae wrote the particular gloss to which reference is made, Clement had not issued this decree.

The first instance of the praescription of any particular form for a rescript is found in legislation enacted by Boniface VIII. In one of his decretals he demands that those who, while they were in Rome, received a promotion, a confirmation in office, a consecration, or a benediction, had to abstain, under pain of invalidity, from taking possession of their offices unless and until they could produce written evidence of this promotion, confirmation, consècration, or blessing.[78]

---

74 C. 7, *de rescriptis,* I, 3, in VI°.

75 C. 23, *de praebendis et dignitatibus,* III, 4, in VI°; c. 4, *de praebendis et dignitatibus,* III, 2, in Clem.

76 Abbas (Nicolaus de Tudeschis), *Omnia Quae Extant Commentaria in Decretales* (5 vols. in 7, Venetiis, 1588), ad c. 8, X, *de rescriptis,* I, 3, n. 5.

77 C. 4, *de rebus ecclesiae alienandis vel non,* III, 2, in Clem.

78 C. 1, *de electione et electi potestate,* I, 3, in Extravag. Com.

CHAPTER II

TRIDENTINE AND POST-TRIDENTINE LAW

The Council of Trent (1545-1563) marked the close of the voluminous decretal law, and, in general, set a stamp of approval and stability on most of that legislation. The Council, at least in so far as the laws on the conferral of offices and benefices were concerned, approved rather than changed the existing legislation, and handed it over to the judicial and coercive power of the Church for interpretation and application. Nevertheless, if in the centuries between the celebration of the Council of Trent and the advent of the present Code, the law underwent but little evolution, the same cannot be said of the subject of that law.

In the first place, at the time of the Council of Trent and for at least two centuries thereafter, offices without endowments for their incumbents were still practically non-existent. Hence the Council made no distinction between offices and benefices, nor did the post-Tridentine canonists. However, beginning with the French Revolution and continuing thereafter, the Church suffered a great diminution in the number of its benefices.[1]

The first result of this was that the word "office" became the generic term and the word "benefice" became related to it as its species. This predicated relationship between the two now stands recognized in the Code of Canon Law. A second result was the efforts on the part of the authors to distinguish in the former legislation between that which applied to all offices and that which applied to them solely by reason of the temporalities conjoined to them.[2] And thirdly, since in a large measure the endowments of benefices had fur-

[1] Poulet-Raemers, *A History of the Catholic Church* (2 vols., St. Louis: Herder & Co., 1943), II, 339-345. Cf. also Bouix, *Tractatus de Episcopo,* II, c. XXIV, n. 4. In an appeal to Pope Gregroy XVI for the use of a new canonical title in connection with ordinations in Belgium, the Bishop of Bruges stated in 1845 that at most only a third of his clerics were provided with a sufficient patrimony.—S. C. Conc., *Brugen.,* 24 aug. 1850—*Thesaurus Resolutionum Sacrae Congregationis Concilii* (167 vols., Romae, 1718-1908), CIX, 295 (*hereafter cited as Thesaurus*).

[2] Cf. Claeys Bouuaert, *De Canonica Cleri Saecularis Obedientia.* (Lovanii, 1904), pp. 217-219. Wernz (1842-1914) treated both offices and benefices under the title of "offices,' but pointed out the instances in which the laws on them differed.—*Ius Decretalium,* II, nn. 239-837.

nished a reason for the emergence and continued existence of the rights which curtailed the exercise of the ordinary power of conferral, namely, the rights of nomination, presentation, patronage, and election, the extinction of the endowment generally resulted in the extinction of the right. These rights suffered a further diminution in consequence of the spread, to the various European nations, of the principles which derived from the French Revolution,[3] and as a result of the lack of canonical chapters in certain missionary countries.[4]

In the realm of public ecclesiastical law there can be no legislative evolution; there can be only a doctrinal development, that is, a more clarified understanding and a more amplified application of principle. The principle remains the same, namely, the Supreme Pontiff in the whole Church, and the Ordinaries in their jurisdiction, have the ordinary power of the free and full conferral of all ecclesiastical offices. The few developments in law as relating to the actual exercise of this power will be noted in the following articles.

ARTICLE I. THE EXTRAORDINARY COLLATOR

It had been the law that, if the ordinary collator failed to exercise his office within the time prescribed by law, or if he conferred an office upon one disqualified in law for receiving it, or if he conferred an office on unworthy candidate, the right and power of conferral passed *ipso iure* to the hands of an extraordinary collator. Pope St. Pius V modified this law to the extent that the extraordinary collator was obliged to rescind, or to establish the invalidity of, the act of the ordinary collator who knowingly conferred an office on a cleric *de iure* or *de facto* unworthy of it before exercising his power.[5]

---

[3] Poulet-Raemers, *A History of the Catholic Church,* II, 359, 360, 373. 382.

[4] Smith, *Elements of Ecclesiastical Law* (3 vols., Vol. I, 9 ed., 1887, New York: Benziger), I, 51; Smith *Notes on the Second Plenary Council of Baltimore* (New York, 1874), pp. 93-94.

[5] Const. *"In conferendis,"* 18 mart. 1567, § 7—*Codicis Iuris Canonici Fontes cura Emi Petri, Card. Gasparri editi* (9 vols., Romae [postea Civitate Vaticana]: Typis Polyglottis Vaticanis, 1923-1939 [Vols. VII-IX *ed cura et studio Emi Iustiniani Card. Serédi*]), n. 119 (hereafter cited as *Fontes*)..

ARTICLE II. THE QUALITIES OF THE RECIPIENT

A. *The Concursus*

The Fathers of the Council of Trent, considering the numerous requisites for the various offices as enunciated in the Decretals, formulated the general rule that, under pain of invalidity of the act of conferral, there be present in the recipient of an office all the qualifications which were demanded by universal or particular law, or by the law of foundation.[6] The Council did not invoke any distinction in order to point to qualifications whose presence was essential for validity, whose absence constituted grounds for recission, and whose verification was a matter of simple recommendation.

A special instrument, the *concursus,* was approved by the Council as a proper aid for determining the qualifications of candidates for offices which were invested with the care of souls.[7] This method of determination was confirmed and the enactments of law underlying it were amplified by an unusually large number of papal constitutions and encyclical letters.[8] While a more ample treatment of this form of examination of candidates for offices invested with the care of souls would find its proper place in a study of the appointment of pastors, there are two points worthy or note in connection with the present discussion. The first is that even the rules of this *concursus* left to the Ordinary the final judgment as to which candidate was to be regarded as the more worthy among those established as worthy.[9] Recourse against the decision of the Ordinary was allowed *in devolutivo tantum.*[10] Wernz, in commenting on this point, stated that if an office without the care of souls was conferred upon a worthy cleric, even though some other cleric had qualified as a more worthy candidate,

---

6 Conc. Trident., sess. XXII, *de ref.*, c. 4; sess. XXV, *de ref.*, c. 5.

7 Conc. Trident., sess. XXIV, *de ref.*, c. 18.

8 E. g., Innocentius XIII, const. "*Apostolici ministerii,*" 23 maii 1723—*Fontes,* n. 280; Benedictus XIII, const. "*In supremo,*" 23 sept. 1724—*Fontes,* n. 283; Benedictus XIV, ep. encycl. "*Ubi primum,*" 3 dec. 1740—*Fontes,* n. 304; Benedictus XIV, const. "*Cum illud,* 14 dec. 1742—Codex I. C., Documentum IV.

9 Conc. Trident., sess. XXIV, *de ref.*, c. 18; Benedictus XIV, const. "*Cum illud,*" 14 dec. 1742, § 11—Codex I. C., Documentum IV.

10 Benedictus XIV, const. "*Cum illud,*" 14 dec. 1742, § 15—Codex I. C., Documentum IV.

such an action did not provide a juridical basis for a rescission of the act whereby the office was conferred.[11]

The second point is that the requirement of the *concursus* never became a universal law because of contrary customs and privileges in certain countries. The Second Plenary Council of Baltimore (1866) referred to the impossibility of fulfilling its requirements in the United States.[12] The III Plenary Council of Baltimore (1884) decreed that the rules of the *concursus* be followed substantially in the appointing of irremovable rectors.[13] But this latter provision was abrogated on June 24, 1931, by a decree of the Sacred Congregation of the Council, transmitted to the Archbishops and Bishops of the United States through His Excellency the Apostolic Delegate.[14]

B. *Order Requisite for the Care of Souls*

Decretal legislation had insistetd that ecclesiastical offices be conferred only upon clerics; however, in regard to the appointment to offices invested with the care of souls, there was a discrepancy in the law. The law was that a cleric could receive an office invested with the care of souls at the age of twenty-five, provided that he receive ordination to the priesthood within one year; yet at the same time a cleric was forbidden to receive ordination to the priesthood before his thirtieth year of age. The Council of Trent eliminated this discrepancy by renewing the prescription that a cleric could receive an office invested with the care of souls only upon the completion of his twenty-fourth year of age,[15] provided that he receive ordination to the priesthood within one year,[16] and by reducing the age required for the reception of the priesthood from thirty to twenty-five.[17]

The question as to the possession of what order was necessary in the

---

[11] *Ius Decretalium*, II, n. 311.

[12] *Concilii Plenarii Baltimorensis II, in Ecclesia Metropolitana Baltimorensi, a die VII. ad diem XXI. Octobris, A. D. MDCCCLXVI, Habiti, et a Sede Apostolica Recogniti, Acta et Decreta* (edito altera, Baltimore, 1894), n. 126.

[13] *Acta et Decreta Concilii Plenarii Baltimorensis III, A. D. MDCCCLXXXIV* (Baltimorae, 1886), n. 36.

[14] Bouscaren, *The Canon Law Digest* (2 vols., Milwaukee: Bruce, 1934-1943), I, 249, under canon 459.

[15] Conc. Trident., sess. XXIV, *de ref.*, c. 12.

[16] Conc. Trident., sess. XXII, *de ref.*, c. 4.

[17] Conc. Trident., sess XXIII, *de ref.*, c. 12.

candidate at the actual moment of his appointment to an office invested with the care of souls is not clear. The controversy, namely, whether the decretal *Si pro clericis* of Boniface VIII[18] constituted merely an exception to the decretal *Praeterea licet* of Alexander III which had required that the candidate be at least a subdeacon,[19] or whether the decretal of Boniface VIII abrogated entirely the decretal of Alexander III, was kept alive among the post-Tridentine commentators. Among those who were of the opinion that an office invested with the care of souls could be conferred only upon one who was at least a subdeacon were Fagnanus (1598-1678),[20] Van Espen (1648-1728),[21] and Schmalzgrueber, (1663-1735).[22] Van Espen cited Rebuffus (1487-1557) as holding the opposite opinion, namely, that an office invested with the care of souls could be conferred upon any cleric, even though he was not constituted even in minor orders. To this latter opinion both Garcia (†ca. 1613)[23] and, in quite recent times, Wernz lent their approval.[24] Neither of these opinions received any vindication in the Code, for the present law enacts that an office invested with the care of souls can be conferred only upon a priest; otherwise the conferral is invalid.[25]

---

18 C. 8, *de praebendis et dignitatibus,* III, 4, in VI°.

19 C. 5, X, *de aetate et qualitate et ordine praeficiendorum* I, 14; JL, n. 14219.

20 *Commentaria in Quinque Libros Decretalium* (5 vols. in 3, Coloniae Allobrogum, 1759), lib. I, tit. XIV, n. 4.

21 *Ius Ecclesiasticum Universum* (5 vols., Lovanii, 1753), pars II, sect. III, tit. II, n. XI.

22 Lib. I, tit. XIV, n. 7.

23 *Tractatus de Beneficiis* (Coloniae Allobrogum, 1636), pars VII, c. I, n. 15.

24 *Ius Decretalium,* II, n. 300.

25 Can. 154.

CANONICAL COMMENTARY

CHAPTER III

PRELIMINARY NOTES

ARTICLE I. THE CONCEPT OF AN ECCLESIASTICAL OFFICE

There is in the Church a twofold power, that of orders and that of jurisdiction, the former for providing men with the supernatural means of salvation, the latter for ruling and governing men toward the attainment of perfect happiness.[1] By divine institution these two powers exist in the Church in hierarchies, that is, the clergy participate in them in various degrees. The hierarchy of orders is composed of bishops, priests, and ministers;[2] that of jurisdiction is composed of the Supreme Pontiff and subordinate bishops.[3] By ecclesiastical institution, however, the hierarchy of jurisdiction has been augmented by additional offices, the incumbents of which partake in varying degrees in the power inherent in the Supreme Pontificate or in the episcopate which is subordinated to it.[4]

There are manifold differences between the power of orders and that of jurisdiction, both in the mode of their acquisition and in the manner of their exercise. But, for the development of the concept of an ecclesiastical office, the pertinent distinction looks primarily to the mode of acquisition. By sacred ordination alone is the power of orders acquired; the power of jurisdiction, however, is acquired either through the divine law itself upon the completion of a legitimate election and the acceptation thereof, which applies to the Supreme Pontiff alone,[5]

---

1 Ottaviani, *Institutiones Iuris Publici Ecclesiastici* (2. ed., 2 vols., Typis Polyglottis Vaticanis, 1935-1936), I, n. 112; St. Thomas Aquinas, *Summa Theologica* (*Opera Omnia,* 32 vols., Parisiis: Vives, 1871-1879), 2a 2ae, 39, a. 3.

2 Can. 108, § 3.

3 Can. 108, § 3.

4 Wernz, *Ius Decretalium,* II, n. 4; Maroto, *Institutiones Iuris Canonici ad Norman Novi Codicis* (2 vols., Madrid: Editorial del Corazon de Maria, 1918), I, n. 486.

5 Can. 109. Maroto uses the phrase *deputatio rite peracta* to designate the reception of supreme jurisdiction upon the acceptation of a legitimate papal election.—*Institutiones,* I, n. 487.

or through a canonical mission, that is, in consequence of the legitimate mandate of a superior.[6]

Thus, in the Church, the Supreme Pontiff has by divine institution supreme jurisdiction over the entire Church and the members thereof;[7] likewise by divine institution bishops, upon receiving their canonical mission from the Pontiff, rule that territory or those persons over whom they are established, but not without being subject to him who has the plenitude of jurisdiction.[8] And by ecclesiastical institution others have been established as participating in this power, and as receiving that participation also through a canonical mission, which is to be exercised in subjection to, and with dependence on, the superior grades of jurisdiction.[9] Such a subordinated grade of jurisdiction, when perpetually established, identified the primary, strict, and objective meaning of a sacred office in the law prior to the Code. Hence an office in this sense was defined by Wernz as a

> *gradus quidam iurisdictionis ecclesiasticae quoad personas, causas, locum, legibus Christi vel Ecclesiae in perpetuum ita institutus, ut iura et onera spiritualia ipsi adnexa nomine proprio et ratione quadam stabili sint exercenda.*[10]

The concept of an ecclesiastical office as defined in the Code is substantially the same as that of the former legislation. The classification of offices however, has been simplified. There are now: a) offices in the broad sense; b) offices in the strict sense; and c) benefices.

a) An office in the broad sense is any employment or function whatsoever which is legitimately practiced for the attainment of a spiritual end.[11] It does not necessarily contain any ecclesiastical power

---

[6] Can. 109.

[7] Can. 218, §§ 1, 2; cf. also Conc. Vatican., sess. IV, c. III, *de vi et ratione primatus Romani Pontificis*—Denzinger-Bannwart-Umberg, *Enchiridion Symbolorum definitionum et declarationum de rebus fidei et morum* (21.-23. ed., Friburgi Brigoviae: Herder & Co., 1937), n. 1831 (hereafter cited as *Enchiridion*.

[8] Can. 329, § 1; cf. also Conc. Vatican., sess. IV, c. III, *de vi et ratione primatus Romani Pontificis*—Denzinger-Bannwart-Umberg, *Enchiridion*, n. 1827; Solieri, *Institutiones Iuris Ecclesiastici* (2. ed., Romae: Pustet, 1921), p. 273.

[9] Ottaviani, *Institutiones*, I, n. 222.

[10] *Ius Decretalium*, II, n. 240, § 2.

[11] "Officium ecclesiasticum lato sensu est quodlibet munus quod in spiritualem finem legitime exercetur: . . ."—Can. 145, § 1.

of orders, of jurisdiction, or of administration, and hence can be conferred upon lay persons, both men and women, as well as upon clerics.

A few examples of such offices explicitly mentioned in the Code are those of notaries,[12] judicial messengers,[13] and all offices within communities of women religious.

b) An office in the strict sense is defined by the Code as a function established by divine or ecclesiastical authority, permanent in character, to be conferred in the form and under the conditions prescribed by the sacred canons, and implying some participation in ecclesiastical power either of orders or of jurisdiction.[14] An office in the strict sense, therefore, embraces not only a grade of, or participation in, the power of jurisdiction, but also—and herein the Code amplifies the concept of an office in relation to the same concept in the former legislation—any position which has attached to it a participation in the power of orders. Even so, the authors almost unanimously agree that the power which inheres in an ecclesiastical office in the strict sense is primarily and principally a power of jurisdiction.[15]

Of the five constituent elements of a sacred office in the strict sense, namely, a spiritual function, divine or ecclesiastical institution, perpetuity, canonical assignment, and participation in the power either of orders or of jurisdiction, two have given rise to differences of opinion among canonists.

With respect to the stability or perpetuity demanded of an office, Maroto (1875-1937)[16] and Cocchi[17] seem to require that this element

---

12 Can. 347, § 1.

13 Can. 1591, § 2.

14 "Officium ecclesiasticum . . . stricto autem sensu est munus ordinatione sive divina sive ecclesiastica stabiliter constitutum, ad norman sacrorum canonum conferendum, aliquam saltem secumferens participationem ecclesiasticae potestatis sive ordinis sive iurisdictionis."—Can. 145, § 1.

15 De Meester, *Juris Canonici et Juris Canonico-Civilis Compendium* (3 vols. in 4, ed. nova, Brugis: Sumptibus et Typis Societatis Sancti Augustini, 1921-1928), I, n. 394, § 2, d (hereafter cited as *Compendium*); Chelodi, *Ius de Personis iuxta Codicem Iuris Canonici* (2. ed., Tridenti: Libr. Tridentum, 1927), n. 131; Wernz-Vidal, *Ius Canonicum ad Codicis Normam Exactum* (7 vols. in 8, Vol. 11, 2. ed., 1928; Vol. VI, 1927; Romae, Apud Aedes Universitatis Gregorianae), II, n. 140, III.

16 *Institutiones,* I, n. 583.

17 *Commentarium in Codicem Iuris Canonici* (5 vols. in 8, Vol. II, 3. ed., Taurinorum Augustae: Marietti, 1930), II, n. 62 (hereafter cited as *Commentarium*).

be present in offices *in specie* as well as *in genere.* They state that a canonical assignment of office, by which alone offices in the strict sense can be obtained, consists of four elements, one of which is a true conferral of title, an absolute, definite, and perpetual concession. This element, they further declare, excludes any temporary, provisional, or merely administrative concession of an office when it is vacant or impeded *de iure* or *de facto.* As it stands, this contention would place such offices as those of vicars capitular, parochial administrators, etc., outside the realm of offices in the strict sense. But the majority of authors holds that the stability required has reference only to the constitution of a position or office *in genere,* that is, that the note of perpetuity does not necessarily imply for any one individual office of its class a continuity of operative effect.[18]

It is true that a vicar capitular does not receive title to a diocese as bishop thereof; on the other hand, there is no inconsistency in holding that he does receive to the diocese a title as vicar capitular, temporary by its very nature, but none the less real. And the same is true of all offices which the Code provides in lieu of those that are vacant or impeded.

Secondly, the power or right which inheres in an office is something that is obtained *ipso facto* by the acqusition of the office itself. If then this is true, how can the power of orders which is acquired once for all through ordination be said to be acquired through an ecclesiastical office? A number of authors either explicitly or implicitly state that any participation in the power already received suffices, and as examples they cite the celebration of Mass, the recitation of the breviary, and the

---

[18] E. g.: "Officium stricte dictum his notis distinguitur: . . . stabile est, stabilitate sc. obiectiva, ita ut ex institutione Christi aut iure ecclesiastico constituatur in Ecclesia modo perpetuo certus potestatis spiritualis gradus, certus iurium spiritualium complexus clerico conferendus aut semper aut quotiens adiuncta iure definita recurrunt, puta munus episcopi, Vicarii Capitularis, administratoris dioecesis, etc. . . ."—Vermeersch-Creusen, *Epitome Iuris Canonici* (3 vols., Vol. I, 6. ed., 1937; Vol. II, 5. ed., 1934; Vol. III, 5. ed., 1936, Romae, Mechliniae. H. Dessain), I, n. 277 (hereafter cited as *Epitome*); Ojetti, *Commentarium in Codicem Iuris Canonici* (4 vols., Vol IV, 1931, Romae: Apud Aedes Universitatis Gregorianae), IV, 3, nota 1; Wernz-Vidal, *Ius Canonicum,* II, n. 140, III; Claeys Bouuaert-Simenon, *Manuale Juris Canonici* (3 vols., Vol. I, 3. ed., Gandae et Leodii: Dessain, 1930), I, n. 306 (hereafter cited as *Manuale*).

like.[19] This participation in the power of orders or of a spiritual function, however, must exist as something distinct from what is the common obligation or privilege of all ordained clerics,[20] and hence must comprehend more than a mere private celebration of Mass or a private recitation of the breviary.

A greater difficulty arises when one seeks to determine the nature of the power which must inhere in some fixed function or abiding charge if it is to exist in the nature of an office in the strict sense. Canon 145, § 1, demands a participation in the power of jurisdiction without determining whether this participation will be in the nature of ordinary or of delegated power. In the absence of such specific determination numerous canonists hold that a participation through the exercise of delegated jurisdictional powers is sufficient.[21]

But in the writer's opinion, the more cogent arguments are on the side of those who hold that the essential concept of an ecclesiastical office in the strict sense embraces ordinary power which is determined by law, so that he who obtains the office obtains also the power inherent in it, apart from any positive act of the superior to supply it, and as its incumbent continues to hold that power, subject in no way to forfeiture or reduction at the will of the superior.[22]

Canon 145 in itself does not expressly postulate ordinary power for the content of an ecclesiastical office whose powers are exclusively of a jurisdictional character. But when this canon is considered in conjunction with canon 197, § 1,[23] then it seems necessary to grant

---

19 Maroto, *Institutiones*, I, n. 579, e; De Meester, *Compendium*, I, n. 394, § 2, d; Chelodi, *Ius de Personis*, n. 131; Cocchi, *Commentarium*, II, n. 59, 2°.

20 Wernz-Vidal, *Ius Canonicum*, II, n. 140, 3°.

21 E. g., Vermeersch-Creusen, *Epitome*, II, n. 742; McBride, *Incardination and Excardination of Seculars*, The Catholic University of America Canon Law Studies, n. 145 (Washington, D. C.: The Catholic University of America Press, 1941), p. 445; Sipos, "Ad officium sacrum an requiritur potestas ordinaria?"—*Jus Pontificium* (Romae, 1921 -), XVI (1936), 67; Blat, *Commentarium Textus Codicis Iuris Canonici* (5 vols. in 7, Vol. II, De Personis, 2. ed., Romae: Collegio "Angelico," 1921), II, n. 446 (hereafter cited as *Commentarium*).

22 Wernz, *Ius Decretalium*, II, n. 240, § 2; Wernz-Vidal, *Ius Canonicum*, II, n. 140, § 3; Maroto, *Institutiones*, I, n. 579, c.; Chelodi *Ius de Personis*, n. 131; Cappello, *Summa Iuris Canonici*, I, n. 271; Prummer, *Manuale Iuris Canonici* (3. ed., Friburgi Brisgoviae: Herder & Co., 1922), q. 72, 3; Coronata, *Institutiones Iuris Canonici* (5 vols., Vol. I, 2. ed., 1939; Vol. III, 1933, Taurini; Marietti), I, n. 426.

23 "Potestas iurisdictionis ordinaria ea est quae ipso iure adnexa est officio."

that the jurisdictional power which inheres in an office is inevitably of the character of ordinary power.

In arguing for the sufficiency of delegated power, both Sipos[24] and McBride[25] acknowledge the function of a synodal judge as an ecclesiastical office in the strict sense, despite the fact that he enjoys only delegated power. They conclude from this that his delegated power constitutes sufficient jurisdictional content for his office. But Hilling points out that the appointment of a synodal judge simply implies a recognition of the qualifications which are demanded of the one who will receive delegated power when he is constituted as a judge in a tribunal for a definite case or cases. From this Hilling concludes that the function of synodal judge is an ecclesiastical office only in the wide sense.[26]

Since only offices in the strict sense are subject to canonical enactments which govern the assignment of ecclesiastical offices,[27] a brief attempt will be made to determine, for practical purposes, which offices of the diocesan curia are offices in the strict sense. On the basis of the conclusion reached, there can be little, if any, doubt about the offices of vicar capitular, of canons of cathedral and collegiate chapters, of diocesan administrators, of vicars general, of *officiales* and *vice-officiales*, of diocesan consultors, of vicars forane, of pastors, of parish vicars, administrators, and substitutes, of rectors of churches, and of rectors of seminaries.

McBride has questioned the office of diocesan chancellor on the grounds that the incumbent does not participate in the power of jurisdiction.[28] This involves a point regarding the exact connotation of the term "jurisdiction." In ecclesiastical law the term refers to the fulness of the power of ruling, whether it exists as a legislative, as an executive and administrative, or as a judicial and interpretative function.[29] That the term is employed in this extensive use in the Code is evidenced by the use of *regimen* as a synonym.[30] Understanding the term "jurisdic-

---

24 "Ad officium sacrum an requiritur potestas ordinaria?"—*Jus Pontificium,* XVI (1936), 67.

25 *Incardination and Excardination of Seculars,* p. 446.

26 "Kirchliches *officium und potestas ordinaria,*"—*Archiv fur katholisches Kirchenrecht* (Innsbruck, 1857-1861; Mainz, 1862-), CXVII (1937), 433.

27 Can. 145, § 2.

28 *Incardination and Excardination of Seculars,* p. 143.

29 Pruemmer, *Manuale Iuris Canonici,* p. 119.

30 Can. 196; cf. Roberti, *De Processibus* (2 vols., Romae: Apud Aedes Facultatis Iuridicae ad S. Apollinaris, 1926), I, n. 38.

tion" in this sense, then there should be no hesitancy in holding with Prince,[31] Coronata,[32] and Maroto,[33] that the position of diocesan chancellor is an office in the strict sense.

The offices of parochial adjutant (*vicarius adiutor*) and of assistant pastor (*vicarius cooperator*), in consequence of the elasticity of function given them by law, have merited considerable discussion. The solution seems to lie, not in placing them definitely in either category of offices, but in holding that their nature can be determined only in the light of the special background in which the specific function is constituted.

All diocesan offices other than those listed above, as well as other minor positions and functions explicitly named by the Code, must be considered offices in the wide sense, and hence not subject to the general norms which govern the assignment to ecclesiastical offices.

c) Benefices as such do not fall within the scope of this work. Canon 1409 describes an ecclesiastical benefice as a juridical entity permanently established or erected by competent ecclesiastical authority, and consisting of a sacred office together with the right of receiving the revenue from the endowment attached to the office.[34]

The office is the foundation of the benefice.[35] In explaining the nature of that office canonists identify it with the "ecclesiastical office" which is described in the fourth title of the second book of the Code.[36] Hence, precisely for the reason that benefices are at the same time ecclesiastical offices, the conferring of them will be governed by the norms with which this work proposes to deal. That which is peculiar to them as benefices does not call for consideration or discussion in the present study.

---

31 *The Diocesan Chancellor,* The Catholic University of America Canon Law Studies, n. 167 (Washington D. C.: The Catholic University of America Press, 1942), p. 44.

32 *Institutiones,* I, n. 426.

33 *Institutiones,* II, n. 742.

34 "Beneficium ecclesiasticum est ens iuridicum a competente ecclesiastica auctoritate in perpetuum constitutum seu erectum, constans officio sacro et iure percipiendi reditus ex dote officio adnexos."

35 Reiffenstuel, *Jus Canonicum Universum* (5 vols. in 7, Venetiis, 1735), lib. III. tit. V, n. 10.

36 Pistocchi, *De Re Beneficiali,* p. 43; Cappello, *Summa Iuris Canonici,* II, n. 470; De Meester, *Compendium,* III, n. 322.

ARTICLE II. FREE CONFERRAL

Canonical assignment of office comprises four essential elements, namely, a) a true concession of title; b) to an ecclesiastical office in the strict sense; c) by a competent ecclesiastical authority; d) according to the norms of the sacred canons.[37] *In actu* it involves three juridical acts: 1) the designation of the person who is to receive the office; 2) the vesting in that person of the title to the office with its rights and duties; and 3) his installation in office. The first act may be termed the material element. It may take place by direct appointment, by nomination, by presentation, by postulation, or by election. The second act is the formal element which is always effected by competent ecclesiastical authority. The third act has proper place only in the conferring of benefices and is but the extrinsic and unessential complement to the juridical act of assignment of office.[38]

There are five types of canonical assignments of office mentioned in the Code: a) free conferral (*libera collatio*);[39] b) presentation or nomination and installation (*per institutionem si praecesserit praesentatio a patrono aut nominatio*); c) confirmation of one that has been elected (*per confirmationem si praecesserit electio*); d) admission of one that has been postulated (*per admissionem si praecesserit postulatio*); e) acceptance of an election of which no confirmation is required (*per simplicem electionem et electi acceptationem, si electio non egeat confirmatione*).[40] The specific element which distinguishes free conferral from the other modes of canonical assignment of office is the unrestricted and full right in virtue of which the proper authority unites the two juridical acts of designation of person and concession of title in one act proper to himself. It is free as opposed to necessary in that the person to whom the office is given has no previous *ius ad rem* acquired by election, presentation, nomination, or other legitimate

[37] Can. 147, § 2.

[38] Maroto, *Institutiones*, I, nn. 585, 604.

[39] In the course of a certain decision the Sacred Congregation of the Council called attention to the fact that the Code consistently uses the expression *institutio canonica* to designate the necessary conferring of an office (after the presentation or nomination of a candidate), and reserves the term *collatio* to designate a free conferring of office. In illustration of the point the Sacred Congregation cited canons 148, 149, 332, 1466, 1467, 1468, etc.—*Acta Apostolicae Sedis, Commentarium Officiale* (Romae, 1909 -), XIV (1922), 459 (hereafter cited as *AAS*); reported in Bouscaren, *The Canon Law Digest*, I, 140, under canon 148.

[40] Can. 148, § 1.

method. It is full in that the person to whom it is given has not been determined by others as in the event of a postulation.[41] It is, therefore, the form of conferral that is most in accord with the nature of the Church.[42]

The third juridical act, namely, installation in office, may rest by law, privilege, prescription, or custom, in the hands of some one other than the authority competent for the conferral without derogating from the right of free conferral.[43]

On the other hand, this freedom on the part of the one conferring an office is by no means absolute. In the first place, it may be dependent in law on what may be called an extrinsic influence, as, for example, supplication or commendation,[44] or on the so called *concursus*, which in certain regions has application in the determination of the recipients of offices to which is annexed the care of souls.[45] Secondly, the one who is to designate the recipient and to vest the title to the office may be obliged by law, legitimate custom, prescription, or privilege, to obtain the counsel or consent of some other person, physical or moral.[46] In the third place, the proper ecclesiastical authority is restricted in the exercise of his right of free conferral of offices not only by the particular laws which have reference to the individual offices, but also by the general norms of canons 150 and 151 and especially by the norms of the canons comprised under the article of the Code entitled "*De libera collatione.*"

Prior to the Code there existed an opinion which seems to have been formulated by Riganti (1661-1735), to the effect that the power of

---

41 Maroto, *Institutiones,* I, n. 604; Coronata, *Institutiones,* I, n. 208; Augustine, *A Commentary on the New Code of Canon Law* (8 vols., Vol. II, 6. ed., St. Louis: Herder, 1936), II, 106.

42 "Libera collatio est modus provisionis canonicae qui maxime principiis dogmaticis et iuridicis de constitutione Ecclesiae congruit."—Coronata, *Institutiones,* I, n. 209, § 1.

43 Maroto, *Institutiones,* I, n. 604.

44 The method followed by the hierarchy of the United States in listing the names of men qualified for the office of bishop is a method of commendation; cf. S. C. Consist., 26 iul. 1916.—*AAS,* VIII (1916), 400.

45 Cf. can. 459, § 4; Benedictus XIV, const. "*Cum illud,*" 14 decembris 1742.—Codex I. C., Documentum IV.

46 "Libera collatio generatim ab unica persona fit, at nihil obstat quominus haec persona procedere teneatur cum consilio, aut etiam cum consensu aliarum personarum; primum verificatur in collatione canonicatuum (can. 403), alterum in collatione officiorum religiosorum ex statutis aliquarum religionum." —Coronata, *Institutiones,* I, n. 219, § 1.

conferral of offices was not a power of jurisdiction.[47] This opinion the Sacred Congregation of the Council cited in a response as recent as the year 1898.[48] Although Schmalzgrueber (1663-1735) stated explicitly that conferral is a power not of orders but of jurisdiction, yet, perhaps as a concession to the opinion of Riganti as a contemporary, he added "*vel potius officii episcopalis*."[49] Sanguinetti (1829-1893) stated that it is a power which pertains to those who have episcopal jurisdiction.[50]

There seems to be little that can be adduced in vindication of Riganti's opinion. In its present canonical use the term "jurisdiction" has a much more extensive significance than it had according to its original meaning in Roman Law. In Roman Law usage jurisdiction implied merely the official act of declaring subjective rights and duties relative to the law. Its use was therefore restricted to the judicial authority in the modern sense,[51] although there is evidence of a late tendency in Roman Law towards a less restricted use of the word to designate a somewhat general administrative power.[52]

It was rather in this latter sense that the Church adopted the term. Since the time of Gregory the Great (590-604), although in canonical terminology from the seventh to the twelfth century the word itself is not of frequent occurence,[53] it has, when employed by canonists, consistently denoted the whole power of government inherent in a juridically perfect society, civil or ecclesiastical.[54] Nominally, then, ecclesiastical jurisdiction comprises the entire social power (*regimen*) of the

---

47 " . . . sive auctoritates, sive exempla, sive rationum momenta expendantur, affirmari debet beneficiorum collationem nihil commune habere cum iurisdictione, neque ad legem iurisdictionis pertinere."—*Commentaria in regulas, constitutiones, et ordinationes cancellariae apostolicae* (opus posthumum, 4 vols. in 2, Coloniae Allobrogum, 1751), ad regul. II, pars III, n. 44.

48 *Potentina*, 16 iul. 1898.—*Thesaurus*, CLVII, 573.

49 Lib III, tit. V, n. 41.

50 *Iuris Ecclesiastici Privati Institutiones* (Romae, 1884), n. 314.

51 "La giurisdizione nel diritto romano era esclusivamente limitata alla decisione delle controversie giuridiche civili."—I. Gluck, *Commentario alle Pandette* (2 vols., Milano, 1888), II, 5.

52 Cf. Van de Kerekhove, "De Notione Iurisdictionis in Iure Romano,"—*Jus Pontificium*, XVI (1936), 49-65.

53 For instances of expressions used synonymously, especially in the councils of the period (e. g., "subjectum habere," "canonice commendatum habere," etc.) cf. Van de Kerekhove, *loc. cit.*

54 "Iurisdictio est potestas publica circa aliorum regimen seu gubernationem."—Reiffenstuel, lib. I, tit. I, n. 29.

Church, whether it exists as a legislative, as an executive and administrative, or as a judicial and interpretative function.[55]

That the term is employed in this extensive meaning in the Code is evidenced by the use of the term *regimen* as synonymous with jurisdiction.[56] It must be concluded, then, with the majority of the recent authors, that even though the Code is not explicit in the matter, the conferring of an office is strictly an act of voluntary, i.e., non-contentious or extra judicial, jurisdiction.[57]

ARTICLE III. ORDINARY AND EXTRAORDINARY RIGHT OF CONFERRAL

Those who possess the right and power to confer offices receive at the hands of the canonists a unique classification which has for its purpose solely and exclusively a technical distinction and clarification. The collators of offices are divided into ordinary and extraordinary, or into those who confer certain offices by ordinary right (*iure ordinario*), and those who confer certain of the same offices by extraordinary right (*iure extraordinario*). The distinction as such is one of public ecclesiastical law. It is not explicitly invoked in the Code.

In the connotations of the two concepts there is no essential consideration of ordinary and delegated power, or of ordinary power that is proper or vicarious; neither is the nature of the office in question a determining factor. The concepts are founded rather on a relative element. The same person may be the ordinary collator of one group of offices, and the extraordinary collator of another office or offices; likewise, some offices will have only an ordinary collator, others will have both an ordinary and an extraordinary. The principles of this classification will become clear from subsequent treatment of its origin and of the individual collators and their offices.

These two concepts, though not exactly with their present connotation, have their inception in papal reservations of benefices[58] and in

---

55 Prummer, *Manuale Iuris Canonici*, p. 119; Ottaviani, *Institutiones*, I, n. 113, p. 218, nota 18.

56 Cf. can. 196.

57 E. g., Wernz, *Ius Decretalium*, II, n. 347; Wernz-Vidal, *Ius Canonicum*, II, n. 235; Coronata, *Institutiones*, I, n. 220, § 2; Beste, *Introductio in Codicem* (Collegeville, Minn.: St. John's Abbey Press, 1938), p. 200 (hereafter cited as *Introductio*).

58 For the beginning of papal reservations cf. Bouix, *Tractatus de principiis iuris canonici* (Parisiis, 1852), p. 182; Thomassinus, *Vetus et Nova Ecclesiae Disciplina circa Beneficia et Beneficarios* (10 vols., Moguntiae, 1787), lib. I, pars II, c. 41, nn. 1-14.

the *ius devolutivum.* To the extent that these two legal norms find place in the Code they remain the chief sources which give rise to the existence of extraordinary collators. In general, the Roman Pontiff is said to be the ordinary collator of all major offices in the Church, the local Ordinary of all minor offices in his jurisdiction, and the major religious superior of all offices in his order of congregation.[59]

Any exception to this general rule gives rise to an extraordinary collator. There are difficulties, however, in the application of this principle, and accordingly, in an attempt to clarify the issue, authors have called upon the aid of other criterions. For instance, Chelodi (1880-1922) stated that the ordinary collator of an office is he who is competent in virtue of the general law or of approved custom to confer the office.[60] On the other hand, Cocchi designates as extraordinary collators those who confer offices in virtue of an apostolic privilege, of legitimate prescription or custom, or of the particular law of the foundation.[61] Finally, Sipos states that the ordinary collator is he who is competent by law, the extraordinary he who is competent by reason of some special title, for example, a superior by reason of the *ius devolutium,* or the Supreme Pontiff by reason of reservation.[62]

It appears to be impossible to formulate any certain criterion that will be applicable in all cases.

---

59 Maroto, *Institutiones,* I, n. 587, D.

60 *Ius de Personis,* n. 134.

61 *Commentarium* II, n. 67, E.

62 *Enchiridion Iuris Canonici* (3. ed., Pecs: "Haladas R. T.," 1936), n. 28, § 4.

CHAPTER IV

THE ORDINARY COLLATOR

Loci Ordinarius ius habet providendi officiis ecclesiasticis in proprio territorio, nisi aliud probetur; . . . — Can. 152.

The Supreme Pontiff and the other bishops constitute by divine law the hierarchy of jurisdiction in the Church.[1] The authority vested in them is absolutely independent of all civil authority.[2] Moreover, in the Pope that authority is complete, supreme, universal, and immediate.[3] It is likewise of a monarchical character in the residential episcopate,[4] even though in this latter instance it is of a subordinate nature.[5] Therefore it is in the offices of the Sovereign Pontiff and of the residential bishop alone that the ordinary right of free and full conferral of ecclesiastical offices inheres by divine law. Hence it is by ecclesiastical law that this right inheres in certain offices other than those of the Supreme Pontiff and residential bishops. Likewise, all rights of election, presentation, and nomination to any office as found in the hands of some other person or persons, clerical or lay, physical or moral, must be acknowledged as deriving from positive legislation, custom, or prescription.[6]

A. *The Pope*

The Supreme Pontiff, by divine law, has the full and free right to the conferral of all offices, vacant or filled, throughout the universal Church. Normally, however, he does not make use of this right to its

1 Can. 108, § 3.

2 Cf. can. 218, § 2; also, Coronata, *Institutiones,* I, nn. 210, 213; Maroto, *Institutiones,* I, n. 587, A.

3 Can. 218, § 1; cf. Conc. Vatican., sess. IV, c. III, *de vi et ratione primatus Romani Pontificis.*—Denzinger-Bannwart-Umberg, *Enchiridion,* n. 1831.

4 Leo XIII, ep. encyl. *"Sapientiae Christianae,"* 10 ian. 1890, n. 19—*Fontes,* n. 605; Benedictus XV, *Epistola ad Delegatum Apostolicum in Indiis Orientalibus,* 15 oct. 1921—*AAS,* XIV (1922), 7; Ottaviani, *Institutiones,* I, nn. 209, 212, 221.

5 Can. 329, § 1; cf. Conc. Vatican., sess IV, c. III, *de vi et ratione primatus Romani Pontificis.*—Denzinger-Bannwart-Umberg, *Enchiridion,* n. 1831.

6 Cf. Schmalzgrueber, lib. III, tit. V, n. 38; Conc. Trident., sess. XIV, *de ref.,* c. 13; Bouix, *Tractatus de Episcopo,* II, cap. I, n. 4; Coronata, *Institutiones,* I, n. 210, § 1; Maroto, *Institutiones,* I, n. 587, A.

full extent.[7] Those matters which pertain to the Church universal antecedent to its diocesan divisions, or which are only indirectly or relatively diocesan in character in as much as they arise consequent to such territorial organization from the relation of the individual dioceses to the central authority, or of one diocese to another, are called *causae maiores* and are reserved to the Pope.[8]

The authors apply the same criterion and terminology to offices. The bishop's power of conferral is limited to offices which are strictly diocesan, that is, in the generic sense that they are occasioned by a diocesan need or are called for in the framework of a diocesan organization. However, the ordinary power of the episcopate lacks competence for certain matters in even this restricted sphere, for there are offices which are occasioned consequent to diocesan organization and yet do not remain exclusively diocesan. The reason is that, while these offices may be immediately conducive to local needs, they serve at the same time a much more extensive purpose and are therefore of such universal import that uniformity in the matter of their assignment is eminently expedient and practically necessary. This uniformity is made possible only through a unified exercise of papal power. The offices, therefore, over which the Pope ordinarily exercises his right of conferral are termed major offices (*officia maiora*); the offices whose conferral rests in the hands of other Ordinaries are called minor offices (*officia minora*).[9]

The following are listed explicitly as major offices over which the Pope exercises his ordinary and proper right of conferral: a) the offices of the cardinals;[10] b) the offices of assessors and secretaries in the Sacred Roman Congregations, the offices of the college of apostolic *protonotaries de numero participantium,* of the auditors of the Roman Rota, of the college of clerics of the Apostolic *Camera*, of the *praelati votantes* of the Apostolic *Signatura*, and the offices of the *praelati referendarii* of the Apostolic *Signatura;*[11] c) the offices of legates;[12] d)

---

[7] Coronata, *Institutiones,* I, n. 209, § 1

[8] Can. 220; cf. Cavagnis, *Institutiones Iuris Publici Ecclesiastici* (2 vols. in 1, Romae, 1882), II, 20.

[9] Maroto, *Institutiones,* I, n. 587, B; Coronata, *Institutiones,* I, n. 213; Beste, *Introductio,* p. 200.

[10] Can. 233.

[11] Pius XI, const. "*Ad incrementum decoris,*" 15 aug. 1934—*AAS,* XXVI (1934), 503-518.

[12] Can. 265.

the offices of bishops[13] of vicars and prefects apostolic,[14] of apostolic administrators[15] and of prelates *nullius*.[16] The reservation, however, of these major offices to the Sovereign Pontiff is not absolute. Numerous exceptions are to be found, particularly in concordats; for example, by the Austrian Concordat of May 1, 1934, there was granted to the metropolitan chapter of Salzburg the right to elect the new Archbishop of Salzburg from three candidates designated by the Holy See.[17]

As Bishop of Rome, the Pope has the same right over the minor offices of that see that other Ordinaries have over minor offices in their sees.

There are other major offices, as, for example, those of the supreme moderators and major superiors of clerical congregations and orders of religious, of abbots of monasteries which are *sui iuris*, of vicars capitular, and of diocesan administrators, the assignment of which rests within the radical right of the Sovereign Pontiff, yet with regard to which prerogatives, rights, and privileges have been accorded to, or obtained by others. For instance, religious orders and congregations have, with but few exceptions, the right of electing their major superiors, and in most instances those who are elected may take office without any confirmation from higher authority.

B. *Residential Bishops*

In virtue of the constitution of the Church as established by Christ, although the Pope is the supreme head, yet he is not the sole authority.[18] The bishops, as the successors of the Apostles, by divine institution, are set over a certain territory, or over a certain portion of the faithful. They exercise their rule with a proper and ordinary legislative, judicial, and coactive power, under the authority of the Supreme Pontiff.[19]

A bishop, when he has been vested with the title to a certain diocese and has taken possession of the diocese, becomes in the proper sense of

---

13 Can. 329, 350.

14 Can. 293.

15 Can. 312.

16 Can. 320.

17 Art. IV, § 1—*AAS*, XXVI (1934), 252; cf. Perugini, *Concordata Vigentia, notis historicis et iuridicis declarata* (Romae: apud Custodiam Librariam Pont. Instituti Utriusque Iuris, 1934), p. 268.

18 "Si Petri eiusque successorum plena ac summa potestas est, ea tamen esse ne putetur sola."—Leo XIII, ep. encycl. "*Satis cognitum*," 29 iun. 1896, n. 25—*Fontes*, n. 630.

19 Cf. can. 108, § 3; 197, § 2; 329, § 1; 335, § 1.

the term an *Ordinarius loci.*[20] In this capacity, but within the limits of his jurisdiction, he has the right of free and full conferral of all minor offices.[21] In virtue of the authority which is inherent in the office he holds, the bishop is not merely the nominal head of the diocese, but the real sovereign over it.[22] It is in his authority that all other diocesan authority strikes its root. He disposes concerning the participation of others in the ecclesiastical authority of the diocese.[23] Accordingly, he confers by ordinary right the various minor offices which reflect this participation in his own episcopal power.

Canonists make use of a particular phrase to describe this right of the local Ordinary. They designate it as a vested legal claim (*intentio in iure fundata*).[24] This designation received legal sanction at a time at least as early as that of Innocent III (1198-1216),[25] and has been retained by the Code in the usage which was vindicated for it at that time, namely, to designate the juridically insinuated and legally intimated right of the bishop to the free conferral of benefices within his jurisdiction.[26]

There exists no reason for not applying the same phrase to a bishop's right of assignment of offices as well as his right of assignment of benefices, and the canonists who wrote after the enactment of the present Code have not hesitated to do so. This *intentio in iure fundata* implies

---

20 Can. 198, § 1.

21 "Loci Ordinarius ius habet providendi officiis ecclesiasticis in proprio territorio, nisi aliud probetur, . . ."—Can. 152.

22 Leo XIII, ep. encycl. "*Sapientiae Christianae,*" 10 ian. 1890, n. 19—*Fontes*, n. 605.

23 "Solus episcopus proprie praelatus ecclesiae dicitur, et ideo ipse solus quasi sponsus annulum ecclesiae recipit, et ideo solus ipse habet plenam potestatem in dispensatione sacramentorum et iurisdictionem in foro causarum quasi persona publica. Alii autem secundum quod ab eo eis committitur."—St. Thomas Aquinas, *Commentarium in IV Libros Sententiarum,* dist. XX, q. I, a. IV, q. 4.

24 "Rem itaque integram et in sua potestate aggrediens Episcopus, libertate sua utatur oportet; ubi iura silent, loco legis est Praesulis auctoritas, praesertim vero quod, ut Doctorum fert adagium, Episcopus intentionem habet in iure fundatam in rebus omnibus quae ad dioecesim suam administrandam attinet."—Leo XIII, const. "*Romanos Pontifices,*" 8 maii 1881, n. 16—*Fontes*, n. 582; Maroto, *Institutiones,* I, n. 587, B; Coronata, *Institutiones,* I, n. 213; Beste, *Introductio,* p. 200; Ottaviani, *Institutiones,* I, n. 220.

25 C. 6, X, *de exceptionibus,* II, 25; Potthast, n. 3791.

26 Can. 1432, § 1.

the same canonical effects as a presumption of law.[27] The meaning and force of the phrase is that the Ordinary's authority is presumed by law to extend to all assignments of office which do not expressly postulate the need of a delegated or vicarious papal power, or regarding which the law does not make an opposite demand. On this principle, those who contest the Ordinary's prerogative in any given case, have the burden of proving their contention by citing the law of a foundation which provides to the contrary, by establishing the existence of a contrary custom, by pointing to the concession of a special privilege, or by vindicating their right as derived through prescription.

C. *Other Local Ordinaries*

Canon 152 declares that local Ordinaries, with the exception of vicars general, have the right of free and full conferral of all offices within their territory.[28] Canon 198, § 1, lists as local Ordinaries, in addition to residential bishops and vicars general, abbots and prelates *nullius*, apostolic administrators, vicars, and prefects, and those who take their place in government when their offices have become vacant by death, transfer, or resignation, or when they are impeded in the exercise of office.

In the main, the distinction between these latter offices and that of a residential bishop is this: whereas the office of a residential bishop has been established and endowed with ordinary jurisdiction proper to the office by divine institution, all others are established by ecclesiastical institution and therefore endowed with ordinary power only by participation in the jurisdiction of the Supreme Pontif or of the residential bishop. The incumbents of these latter offices, however, are given by law the same rights in relation to the minor offices that are given to residential bishops. Therefore canonists attribute to them also the *intentio in iure fundata.* [29] There is no question but that in exercising the right of free conferral these local Ordinaries do so by ordinary right (*iure ordinario*). By provision of ecclesiastical law they are in-

---

27 Coronata, *Institutiones,* III, n. 1273.

28 "Loci Ordinarius ius habet providendi officiis ecclesiasticis in proprio territorio, nisi aliud probetur; hac tamen potestate caret Vicarius Generalis sine mandato speciali."

29 Coronata, *Institutiones,* I, n. 213; Maroto, *Institutiones,* I, n. 605, IV; Beste, *Introductio,* p. 200.

vested with the same rights and powers of governing (*regimen*) that residential bishops have by divine institution.[30]

A word must be said about those who, although designated as local Ordinaries, assume merely by way of temporary provision an office which has been left vacant by the death, transfer, or resignation of the ordinary incumbent, or who exercises the rights of an office and fulfills the duties when the incumbent is impeded. In succeeding the vicar and prefect apostolic the pro-vicar and pro-prefect assume without restriction all the rights, duties, and powers of those whom they succeed.[31] But the same cannot be said of the apostolic administrator given to a diocese merely for a time (*ad tempus*),[32] or of vicars capitular and diocesan administrators. The three of them have the same office with equal rights and duties and the same restrictions on the exercise of their power.[33] Hence, what is said in the following paragraphs of the powers of the vicar capitular will be applicable to the temporary apostolic administrator and the diocesan administrator.

Canon 431, § 1, states that in a case of vacancy the government of the diocese devolves on the cathedral chapter (or the board of diocesan consultors where there are no chapters), unless there be appointed an apostolic administrator or the Holy See has provided otherwise.[34] The nature of the power granted to this board of administration may be ascertained from canon 435, § 1, wherein it is stated that at the vacancy of the bishopric the ordinary jurisdiction of the bishop in temporal and spiritual affairs devolves on the chapter, and it is this same ordinary jurisdiction which passes wholly to the vicar

---

[30] "Vicarii et praefecti Apostolici iisdem iuribus et facultatibus in suo territorio gaudent, quae in propriis dioecesibus competunt Episcopis residentialibus, . . ."—Can. 294, § 1.

"Abbas vel Praelatus *nullius* easdem potestates ordinarias easdemque obligationes cum iisdem sanctionibus habet, quae competunt Episcopis residentialibus in propria dioecesi."—Can. 323, § 1.

[31] Can. 309, § 2.

[32] Can. 315, § 2.

[33] Can. 315, § 2, 1; 431, § 2; cf. also McDonough, *Apostolic Administrators,* The Catholic University of America Canon Law Studies, n. 139 (Washington, D.C.: The Catholic University of America Press, 1941), pp. 91-97.

[34] "Sede vacante, nisi adfuerit Administrator Apostolicus vel aliter a Sancta Sede provisum fuerit, ad Capitulum ecclesiae cathedralis regimen dioecesis devolvitur."

capitular.[35] The vicar capitular, therefore, is the successor of the bishop and not his jurisdictional inferior.[36] He rules the diocese with ordinary legislative, judicial, and coactive power,[37] with but two general restrictions peculiar to his office, namely, he may not do what is expressly forbidden him by law,[38] and *sede vacante nihil innovetur.*[39]

First, does the general norm of canon 436 curtail the exercise of his rights as ordinary collator of diocesan offices? Since the law is taken almost verbatim from the pre-Code law,[40] it is to be interpreted according to the solidly founded doctrine of pre-Code canonists.[41] The clause *ne sede vacante aliquid innovetur* was understood by authors previous to the Code in the sense that no prejudice should be brought to bear either on the Church itself or on the successors to the episcopal see in question. Furthermore, they added, since during a vacancy the Church lacked a legitimate defender, the performance of any acts which brought harm or detriment to the Church itself stood as null and void, but they indicated at the same time that any meritorious acts

---

35 "Sicut ad Capitulum ante deputationem Vicarii Capitularis, ita deinde ad Vicarium Capitularem transit ordinaria Episcopi iurisdictio in spiritualibus et temporalibus, . . ."—Can. 435, § 1.

"In Vicario constituendo nullam sibi iurisdictionis partem Capitulum retinere potest, nec gerendo muneri tempus praefinire aliasve restrictiones praestituere."—Can. 437.

36 Pius IX, const. *"Romanus Pontifex,"* 28 aug. 1873—*Fontes,* n. 565; Cocchi, *Commentarium,* II, n. 343; McDonough, *Apostolic Administrators,,* p. 94; Ayrinhac, *Constitution of the Church in the New Code of Canon Law* (New York, 1925), p. 273; Jaeger, *The Administration of Vacant and Quasi-Vacant Dioceses in the United States,* The Catholic University of America Canon Law Studies, n. 81 (Washington, D.C.: The Catholic University of America, 1936), pp. 163-166.

37 Ryan, *Principles of Episcopal Jurisdiction,* The Catholic University of America Canon Law Studies, n. 120 (Washington, D.C.: The Catholic University of America Press, 1939), pp. 135, 40, 124.

38 Can. 435, § 1.

39 Can. 436.

40 C. 1, X, *ne sede vacante aliquid innovetur,* III, 9.

41 "Canones qui ius vetus ex integro referunt, veteris iuris auctoritate, atque ideo ex receptis apud probatos auctores interpretationibus, sunt aestimandi; . . . " —Can. 6, § 2; cf. also Neuberger, *Canon* 6, The Catholic University of America Canon Law Studies, n. 44 (Washington, D.C.: The Catholic University of America, 1927), pp. 70-72.

were highly recommended and honored wih full validity.[42] Therefore the vicar capitular is prohibited from placing detrimental acts, but is not in any way curtailed in the placing of those which redound to the good of the diocese.[43] Accordingly canon 436 contains no prohibition of the vicar capitular's conferring of offices upon worthy and capable clerics.

Secondly, is it expressly forbidden for vicars capitular to confer ecclesiastical offices? In general, no. He is forbidden to confer offices which are perpetual benefices,[44] and he is also forbidden to confer parishes until the see has been vacant a full year.[45] But other than this there is no express prohibition in this matter in the Code. Therefore, regarding all offices except parishes and perpetual benefices the vicar capitular has the full and free right of conferral.

This conclusion is without direct support on the part of canonists. Coady declares that "when the see is vacant, in the case of *libera collatio* which belongs exclusively to the bishop, ordinary power is not invested in the vicar capitular or diocesan administrator."[46] Chelodi[47] and Cappello[48] are most explicit in stating that the vicar capitular cannot confer offices except in the few cases expressly permitted him by law. It is impossible to reconcile these statements with the wording of canon 435, § 1, which states that he can act with ordinary power in all things not expressly forbidden him.

Authors in the majority avoid making statements as strong as those of Chelodi and Cappello. They imply the same opinion, however, by omitting mention of the conferral of offices in their listing of those

---

42 Reiffenstuel, lib. III, tit. IX, nn. 13-16; Schmalzgrueber, lib. III, tit. IX, nn. 1-14; Wernz, *Ius Decretalium*, II, n. 316; Hermes, *Dissertatio Historico-Canonica de Capitulo Sede Vacante vel Impedita et de Vicario Capitulari* (Lovanii: Valinthout Fratres, 1873), p. 58; De Angelis, *Praelectiones Iuris Canonici* (6 vols., Romae: Ex Typographia della Pace, 1877-1878), III, 9.

43 Blat, *Commentarium*, II, 471-472; Augustine, *A Commentary on the New Code*, II, 489-490.

44 Can. 1432, § 2.

45 Can. 455, § 2, 3°.

46 *The Appointment of Pastors*, The Catholic University of America Canon Law Studies, n. 52 (Washington, D.C.: The Catholic University of America, 1929), p. 108.

47 *Ius de Personis*, n. 136.

48 *Summa Iuris Canonici*, I, n. 281, § 5.

things which are permitted to the vicar capitular.[49] This opinion seems to be based on two points. The first point is that in the canons which deal with the conferral of the individual offices the word *episcopus* is used instead of *loci Ordinarius.*[50] On the basis of this terminology Zaplotnik, for instance, concludes that the vicar capitular is excluded from the conferral of offices.[51] He adduces, however, no legal principle to justify this restricted interpretation of the term *episcopus*. An example of an express prohibition such as is required by canon 435, § 1, may be found in canon 492, § 1, where although the term *episcopus* is used, nevertheless the vicar capitular is explicitly excluded from possessing the competence which the law accords to the bishop.[52]

The second point upon which the authors base their opinion which restricts the right of the vicar capitular is centered in the fact that the law recounts instances in which the vicar capitular may act. For example, canon 426, § 5, states that if a consultor dies or resigns during the vacancy of the see, the vicar capitular (diocesan administrator) may, with consent of the rest of the consultors, appoint another; canon 1573, § 7, states that if the *officialis* is elected to be the vicar capitular, he is to appoint another *officialis;* and canon 455, § 2, 1°, states that the vicar capitulor may appoint parochial vicars, that is, administrators, substitutes, adjutants, and assistants. The authors conclude that these prescripts are a taxative

---

49 E. g., Cocchi, *Commentarium,* II, n. 67; Coronata, *Institutiones,* I, p. 244, nota 4; Castillo, *Disertacion Historico-Canonica sobre la Potestad del Cabildo en Sede Vacante o Impedida del Vicario Capitular,* The Catholic University of America Canon Law Studies, n. 4 (Washington, D.C.: The Catholic University of America, 1919), pp. 76-83; McDonough, *Apostolic Administrators,* pp. 101, 145.

50 E. g., can. 366, § 1; 372, § 1; 404, § 1; 423; 445; 1573, § 1. An exception to this general principal is canon 480, § 1, which states that rectors of churches are freely appointed by the local Ordinary.

51 *De Vicariis Foraneis,* The Catholic University of America Canon Law Studies, n. 47 (Washington, D.C.: The Catholic University of America, 1927), p. 59.

52 "Episcopi, non autem Vicarius Capitularis vel Vicarius Generalis, condere possunt Congregationes religiosas; . . ."

enumeration of the instances in which the vicar capitular may act.[53]

This conclusion does not seem justified. The Code establishes the general principle that the vicar capitular can do all the things which are not expressly forbidden him. The fact that the Code further lists a few specific instances in which he can confer offices does not imply the existence of an express prohibition in all other cases relative to which his capacity is not similarly predicated. It cannot be argued that the positive acknowledgment of his power would be superfluous if the full force of the fundamental principle were conceded. The Code not infrequently repeats prescripts in whole or in part for the purpose of maintaining coherence and of obviating doubts that might arise, and particularly when some further purpose is served as in canon 426, § 5, where it is stated that the vicar capitular needs the consent of the consultors for his act, and in canon 1573, § 7, where it is pointed out that the same person may not be both vicar capitular and *officialis*.

With respect to the individual offices one could grant that canon 426, § 5, specifies the only instance in which a diocesan administrator could appoint a diocesan consultor if the fulfillment of the law were not subject to human execution. But as it is, experience has proved that deficiencies in effective government and administration can be and are at times found, particularly towards the end of an aging bishop's reign. Hence it is not entirely hypothetical to suppose a case in which the diocesan administrator would find a very meagre body of consultors. The Code requires that there be at least six consultors, or, in dioceses which have but very few priests, four.[54] In view of the decree of the Sacred Congregation of the Consistory, issued on February 22, 1919, and effective for three years, in which decree provision was made that for those dioceses which had fewer than five or six consultors the metropolitan or senior suffragan was to appoint the administrator,[55] it would need to be a small diocese indeed in which four consultors would suffice. Now, if upon his assumption of office the diocesan administrator finds that there is a smaller number in consequence of past failure

---

[53] Maroto, *Institutiones*, I, n. 605, IV; Klekotka, *Diocesan Consultors*, The Catholic University of America Canon Law Studies, n. 8 (Washington, D.C.: The Catholic University of America, 1920), p. 55; G. Simenon, "Renuntiatio Officiorum Ecclesiasticorum,"—*Revue Ecclésiastique de Liège* (Leodii, 1908 -), XXII (1930-1931), 185, nota 4.

[54] Can. 425, § 1

[55] *AAS*, XI (1919), 75.

to fill vacancies, or for some other cause, he would have the obligation of remedying such a defect in his senate body, which is called on to offer him assistance in even larger measure than the law demands in relation to the bishop in the proper administration of the diocese. His act would bring no harm or detriment to the diocese, but would be a meritorious one in keeping with the mind of the law.

Canon 1573, § 3, states that if the *officialis* is elected the vicar capitular he is to appoint another *officialis*. Tobin, considering the important duties of this office, states that if the office of *officialis* becomes vacant during the vacancy of the see the vicar capitular is likewise to appoint an incumbent.[56] Similarly, Prince[57] and Lega-Bartoccetti, [58] although canon 372, § 1, states that the chancellor is to be appointed by the bishop, grant to the vicar capitular the right and power of conferring this office.

Hence, while prudence demands that due deference be anticipated with reference to the eventual wishes of the episcopal successor, the vicar capitular is nevertheless empowered to act in the conferral of offices, as in all things else, when the good of the diocese calls for an exercise of this power. The mind of the Church is that offices have proper and suitable incumbents at all times. This is evident from her law that no office is to remain vacant beyond a period of six months.[59] Other than for the appointment of pastors to parishes and of incumbents to perpetual benefices no exception is made to the law regarding the free and full conferral of offices for the period of the vacancy of the see. That law and the right involved in it are of equal application for the bishop and the vicar capitular.

D. *Cardinals*

Cardinal bishops are the proper Ordinaries of their respective suburbicarian dioceses. In their capacity of local Ordinaries they too enjoy the right and power which canon 152 accords. To Cardinal priests and deacons there are assisgned certain churches within the city of Rome which are called titles and deaconries respectively.[60] With re-

---

56 *De Officiali Curiae Dioecesanae* (Romae: Apud Aedes Pontificae Universitatis Gregorianae, 1936), p. 108.

57 *The Diocesan Chancellor,* p. 56.

58 *Commentarius in Iudicia Ecclesiastica* (3 vols., Romae: Anonima Libreria Catolica-Italiana, 1934-1941), I, 148.

59 Can. 155.

60 Can. 231, § 2.

spect to the offices extant in these churches the Cardinals are given the same rights as are attributed by the Code to local Ordinaries.[61] This right the Cardinals enjoyed prior to the Code, but then they held it in virtue of a special privilege. It was for this reason that the authors included them among the extraordinary collators.[62]

Now, however, inasmuch as the common law attributes to them the vested legal claim (*intentionem in iure fundatam*) which entitles them to confer these offices,[63] it seems incongruous to regard them as extraordinary collators in relation to the offices extant in their respective churches. Coronata includes them among the ordinary collators.[64] But this does not seem to be correct since, as was pointed out, the conferral of offices is an act of jurisdiction and canon 240, §2, expressly excludes all jurisdiction over the faithful save in those things which pertain to the discipline, correction or morals, and service of their particular churches.[65] Secondly, the Cardinals cannot confer these offices during their absence from the Curia[66] which they would be able to do if this power which they have is that of voluntary jurisdiction as it is in other ordinary collators. Thirdly, the Sovereign Pontiff is to be preferred as the ordinary collator of offices in the see and city of Rome itself. Therefore it seems necessary to attribute to these Cardinal priests and deacons a right that is quasi-ordinary and with Maroto to designate them as quasi-ordinary collators.[67]

---

[61] Can. 240 § 2; 1432, § 1.

[62] Wernz, *Iu Decretalium,* II, n. 348.

[63] Can. 1432, § 1.

[64] *Institutiones,* I, n. 219, § 2.

[65] "Ceteri Cardinales in suis titulis vel diaconiis, postquam eorundem canonicam possessionem ceperint, omnia possunt quae locorum Ordinarii in suis ecclesiis, exceptis ordine iudiciorum et qualibet iurisdictione in fideles, sed salva potestate in iis quae ad disciplinam, morum correctionem, servitium ecclesiae pertinent."—Can. 240 § 2.

[66] S. C. Conc., 12 iun. 1943—*AAS,* XXXV (1943), 399; reported in*The Jurist* (Washington, D.C., 1941 -), IV (1944), 630.

[67] *Institutiones,* I, n. 605, II.

. same rights as are attributed by the Code to Local Ordinaries.[61]

CHAPTER V

The Extraordinary Collator

The concept of extraordinary collator has, under the present law as under the old, a twofold basis in the papal provision of minor offices and in the *ius devolutivum*.

ARTICLE I. PAPAL ASSIGNMENT OF OFFICE

In virtue of his supreme, full, immediate, and ordinary jurisdiction over the Church, the Roman Pontiff is the supreme and universal authority for the conferring of all ecclesiastical offices both major and minor. He has ordinary right and power over all offices, but when he exercises this prerogative with respect to minor offices outside the see of Rome it is said to be an extraordinary act, even though the authorization for it is sanctioned in the general law.[1] The exercise of the Pontiff's prerogative with respect to the conferral of minor offices may take place in any of four ways:

a) *Iure praeventionis,* whereby the Pope confers a minor office which is not yet vacant, as, for example, through the appointment of an adjutant pastor with the right of succession.[2]

b) *Iure concursus,* whereby with respect to some vacant minor office the Pope exercises or intends to exercise his power of conferral without at the same time placing any obstacle to, or restriction on, the exercise of the right of the ordinary collator.

c) *Iure reservationis,* whereby the Supreme Pontiff reserves to himself to the exclusion of all inferiors the right to confer a certain office or offices either in an individual instance or in all cases.[3]

d) *Iure devolutivo,* whereby the Supreme Pontiff becomes the extraordinary collator of a benefice which by default of the ordinary collator has remained vacant beyond the period of the six months of time available for the appointment of an incumbent in the benefice.[4]

---

1 Maroto, *Institutiones,* I, n. 587, D.

2 Cf. can. 1433.

3 E. g., can. 1435, § 1. For a more detailed study of these types of papal provisions cf. Barraclough, *Papal Provisions,* p. 8 seq.; Haydt, *Reserved Benefices,* pp. 4-6.

4 "Si Ordinarius intra semestre ab habita certa vacationis notitia beneficium non contulerit, huius collatio devolvitur ad Sedem Apostolicam, salvo praescripto can. 458."—Can. 1432, § 3.

In so far as the Code treats of these papal appointments it does so under the heading of benefices. In theory and in practice there is no obstacle, legal or otherwise, to the Pope's using any of these types to make provision for offices which are not benefices. It is but a matter of fact that he does not do so. Hence the norms which govern these types of papal assignment of office must be left for treatment under a consideration other than that of the free conferral of offices.

ARTICLE II. IUS DEVOLUTIVUM

The power of free conferral resides in a human instrument, and is therefore liable to defects in its exercise. These defects consist in the failure to exercise this power when its exercise is demanded, and in exercising it to the detriment of individuals or of the Church as a whole. These defects are generally divided into three categories: a) the fault or negligence of the competent authority in leaving an office vacant beyond the stipulated time; b) the designation of an unworthy candidate as the recipient of the office; and c) the failure to observe the proper norms which govern the act of conferral.[5]

These defects may be found not only in the act of free conferral, but also in the other types of assignment of office. Still they do not have everywhere the effect of calling into play the action of an extraordinary collator. There is no norm in the Code, either general or with respect to a particular office, whereby the power of full and free conferral of an office passes to the hands of an extraordinary from the hands of an ordinary collator in view of the latter's failure to act within the specified limit of time, in view of his designation of an unworthy recipient, or in view of his neglect to observe the canonical norms enacted with reference to the conferring of an office.[6] Nevertheless these defects in other types and methods of assignment of office are attended with the specific sanction of the *ius devolutivum.* The effect of this sanction is the substitution of an extraordinary collator who will have the free and full conferral of the offices in question. A brief study of these laws seems in place here.

---

[5] Cappello, *Summa Iuris Canonici,* I, n. 279; Chelodi, *Ius de Personis,* n. 135, B; Cocchi, *Commentarium,* II, n. 68.

[6] The laws whereby benefices pass from the hands of the ordinary collator because of his fault or negligence in leaving them vacant beyond six months (can. 1432, § 3), or because of simony (can. 1435, § 1, 3°), pertain exclusively to benefices.

With regard to canonical elections, the law lists seven instances in which the sanction of the *ius devolutivum becomes* effective. These instances are recounted in various canons.

1) The first is canon 161. A chapter or body of electors is given an available period of three months' time for exercising its right of election. Upon the expiration of this time the power passes into the hands of an extraordinary collator and the office becomes subject to free conferral[7].

2) The second is canon 166[8] in conjunction with canon 2390, § 2, whereby those electors who solicited or willingly admitted the illegitimate interferencee of laymen or of the secular power are deprived of their right to vote for that instance.[9] In the event that the ones thus deprived constitute a majority of the electors, the body can no longer function as such[10]. Hence the office becomes subject to free conferral by an extraordinary collator[11].

3) The third is canon 2391, § 2, whereby the competent superior is empowered to inflict penalties on those who knowingly neglect the substantial form of election[12]; if this penalty is one of privation of the right to vote and affects the majority of the voters, the superior is to make provision for the office[13].

---

7 "Si cui collegio sit ius eligendi ad vacans officium, electio, nisi aliud iure cautum fuerit, nunquam differatur ultra trimestre utile computandum ab habita notitia vacationis officii; quo termino inutiliter elapso, Superior ecclesiasticus, cui ius confirmandae electionis vel ius providendi successive competit, officio vacanti libere provideat."

8 "Si laici contra canonicam libertatem electioni ecclesiasticae quoquo modo sese immiscuerint, electio ipso iure invalida est."

9 "Quod si electioni a collegio clericorum vel religiosorum peragendae, laici vel saecularis potestas sese illegitime contra libertatem canonicam, immiscere praesumpserint, electores qui hanc immixtionem sollicitaverint vel sponte admiserint, ipso facto privati sunt pro ea vice iure eligendi; . . ."

10 Cf. Parsons, *Canonical Elections,* The Catholic University of America Canon Law Studies, n. 118 (Washington, D. C.: The Catholic University of America Press, 1939) p. 211.

11 'Si electio intra praescriptum tempus peracta non fuerit, aut collegium iure eligendi privetur in poenam, libera officii provisio ad eum Superiorem devolvitur, a quo confirmanda esset electio vel cui ius providendi successive competit."—Can. 178.

12 "Singuli vero electores qui substantialem electionis formam scienter non servaverint, possunt pro gravitate culpae ab Ordinario puniri."

13 Can. 178.

4) The fourth is canon 2391, § 1, whereby the competant superior becomes the extraordinary collator of an office to which a body of electors has elected one who is unworthy[14].

5) The fifth is canon 2392, 2°, whereby those who are guilty of the delict of simony with reference to any and all offices, benefices, or ecclesiastical dignities are deprived forever of their right to vote[15]. The election to the office in which this simony had place is not only invalid[16], but the office itself, in the event that it is a benefice, is in that instance reserved to the Holy See for conferral[17]. If the electors who were innocent of the delict of simony constituted a majority, they of course retain the right of subsequent elections; otherwise the conferral devolves upon the extraordinary collator of canon 178 until such time as a new body of electors is constituted.

6) The sixth is canon 2393. It deprives of their right to vote for that instance those who presume to ignore and pass by the authority of him who has the right of confirmation in office[18].

7) The seventh is canon 2394, 3°. It inflicts a similar penalty, reserved to the Holy See, on those who before seeing his letters of confirmation admit one to office.[19]

With regard to that type or method of assignment of office which the Code designates as postulation the law lists two instances in which the *ius devolutivum* becomes effective. Canon 181, § 2, deprives of their right to vote in that instance a body of electors which fails to forward the postulation to the proper superior within the eight days

---

14 "Collegium quod indignum scienter elegerit, ipso facto privatur pro ea vice iure ad novam electionem procedendi."

15 "Firmo praescripto can. 729, delictum perpetrantes simoniae in quibuslibet officiis, beneficiis aut dignitatibus ecclesiasticis: . . . ipso facto privati in perpetuum manent iure eligendi . . ."

16 Can. 729.

17 Can. 1435, § 1, 3°.

18 "Omnes qui iure eligendi, praesentandi, vel nominandi legitime fruuntur, si, neglecta auctoritate illius cui confirmatio vel institutio competit, officium, beneficium aut dignitatem ecclesiasticam conferre praesumpserint, suo iure pro ea vice ipso facto privati manent."

19 "Capitula vero, conventus aliique omnes ad quos spectat, huiusmodi electos, praesentatos vel nominatos ante litterarum exhibitionem admittentes, ipso facto a iure eligendi, nominandi, vel praesentandi suspensi maneant ad beneplacitum Sedis Apostolicae."

prescribed by law[20], and canon 182, § 1, inflicts a like penalty on those who knowingly postulate one who is subject to an impediment from which a dispensation cannot or is not customarily given[21].

For all of these cases the Code gives the same general rule for determining the extraordinary collator. It is that superior who has power to confirm the election, or, if no confirmation is needed, the one who has the next right to fill the office.[22] Maroto adds that one can also determine the proper superior by ascertaining which superior would have power to remove the person from office or accept his resignation,[23] as an example, the proper superior for these acts with respect to a diocesan congregation of religious would be the local Ordinary.[24]

Finally, the Code designates extraordinary collators for individual offices. For instance, when a cathedral chapter or body of diocesan consultors fails for any reason whatever to elect a vicar capitular or a diocesan administrator within eight days after receiving notice of the vacancy of the see, the power of appointing one passes to the metropolitan, or, if the metropolitan see is vacant, or if a metropolitan and a suffragan see are simultaneously vacant, to the senior suffragan bishop.[25] Moreover, the vicar capitular or diocesan administrator must possess certain qualifications, namely, he must be a priest, at least thirty years of age, and must not have been elected, nominated, or presented for the vacant see;[26] should the one elected fail to have any one of these qualifications the election is invalid, and the power of appointing a vicar capitular or diocesan administrator passes to the one designated above.[27]

---

20 "Si intra praescriptum tempus postulatio missa non fuerit, ipso facto nulla evadit et electores pro ea vice privantur iure eligendi aut postulandi, nisi probent se a mittenda postulatione iusto detentos fuisse impedimento."

21 "Reiecta a Superiore postulatione, ius eligendi ad collegium redit, nisi electores scienter illum postulaverint qui tali detinetur impedimento in quo nequeat aut non soleat dispensari; tunc enim provisio ad Superiorem pertinet."

22 Can. 161; 178.

23 *Institutiones,* I, n. 756.

24 Parsons, *Canonical Elections,* p. 212.

25 "Si Capitulum intra praescriptum tempus Vicarium aut oeconomum, quavis de causa, nullum deputaverit, deputatio ad Metropolitam devolvitur; si autem ecclesia ipsa metropolitana fuerit vacans vel metropolitana et suffraganea, ad antiquiorem ex Episcopis suffraganeis."—Can. 432, § 2.

26 Can. 434, § 1.

27 "Si praescriptae § 1 conditiones posthabitae fuerint, Metropolita, aut si ecclesia metropolitana vacans fuerit, vel de ipso Capitulo metropolitano agatur, antiquior provinciae Episcopus, agnita rei veritate, Vicarium pro ea vice deputet; . . ."—Can. 434, § 3.

There is but one other instance in which a Metropolitan has or acquires by law any right in the conferral of offices in the suffragan sees in his province. That instance occurs in the event that a suffragan bishop fails to confer a benefice upon the one presented by a patron within the available time set by law. Upon the expiration of this time the Metropolitan is given, not the right of freely conferring the benefice, but the right to confer it upon the one presented.[28]

In addition to these laws whereby offices are subject to a type of canonical assignment other than that of free conferral there are laws which restrict the right of free conferral inasmuch as outside persons, physical or moral, are granted the exercise of a prior right of nomination or of presentation. Religious superiors have the right of presenting pastors, parish vicars, adjutants, and assistants in parishes which are entrusted or united to religious houses;[29] those who have rights of patronage are entitled to present clerics for vacant churches and benefices.[30] Should those who have such rights of nomination or presentation knowingly nominate or present an unworthy candidate, they lose their right for that instance,[31] and the local Ordinary may confer the office on whom he will with full freedom.

Likewise, should those who enjoy such rights exceed the limits thereof by ignoring or passing by the authority of him who has right of granting institution in office, then the same penalty would ensue, and it would rest with the local Ordinary to confer the office.[32]

There is an indicated time limit also for the exercise of the rights of patronage with respect to appointment to churches and benefices. Upon the lapse of an available period of four months' time, or even less if it be so prescribed by the law of foundation or by legitimate custom, from the date on which notice of the vacancy or notification of the names of those approved in *concursus* has been received,[33] the rights are *ipso*

---

28 Can. 274, 1°.

29 Can. 456; 471, § 2; 475, § 1; 476, § 4; 480, § 2; 1425, § 1, 2°.

30 Can. 455, 1°.

31 "Clerici vel laici qui indignum scienter praesentaverint vel nominaverint, iure praesentandi vel nominandi ipso facto pro ea vice carent."—Can. 2391, § 3.

32 Can. 2393.

33 Cf. can. 1457.

iure lost and the benefice or church becomes subject to free conferral by the local Ordinary.[34]

It is well to repeat that the right to confer an office, to elect, to postulate, or to present a candidate — with the sole exception of the right of a chapter or body of diocesan consultors to elect a vicar capitular or diocesan administrator—is lost only by default or negligence.[35] The law itself is primarily concerned with the filling of the office, but the exercise of the *ius devolutivum* quite generally connotes the existence of a penalty for the defaulter, so that the default or negligence of the predecessor does not imply for his successor in office the same deprivation of right.[36] Once the conditions established by the law are present, however, the effect of the *ius devolutivum* follows *ipso iure;* not even a declaratory sentence is necessary.

This, in brief, is a summary of the provisions of law in consequence of which the *ius devolutivum* becomes operative for extraordinary collators. From this summary it is evident, first, that the *ius devolutum* becomes operative by law only *per modum actus,* that is, in relation to individual offices in particular cases, and secondly, that the office itself is affected only in so far as it is in a particular case withdrawn from the possibility of any and every mode of assignment other than that of free conferral. In consequence two questions arise. They concern: a) the length of time which is given the extraordinary collator to exercise his right, and b) the extent of his right.

Since one effect of the *ius devolutimu* is to make an office subject to free conferral, it follows that the extraordinary collator is bound by the rule of cannon 155, which stipulates an available period of six months for the conferring of an office. For example, although the body of electors had a period of but three months in which to hold their election, the extraordinary collator will have an additional period of six months in which to act. Canon 155 adds, however, that this six-month period constitutes the legal norm only in relation to those offices for the assignment of which the law has not stipulated a shorter or a longer period of time as the period within which the conferral of the

---

34 "Si intra praescriptum tempus praesentatio facta non fuerit, ecclesia vel beneficium pro eo casu fit liberae collationis."—Can. 1458, § 1.

35 Wernz-Vidal, *Ius Canonicum,* II, n. 220, VIII; Coronata, *Institutiones,* I, n. 208, C; Maroto, *Institutiones,* I, n. 587, E; Capello, *Summa Iuris Canonici,* I, n. 275.

36 Coronata, *Institutiones,* I, n. 208, C; Cappello, *Summa Iuris Caninici,* I, n. 275.

office must be effected. A cathedral chapter or body of diocesan consultors is given eight days in which to fill the office of vicar capitular or diocesan administrator. This certainly appears to be a special prescript directed to a particular office. Even though Maroto holds otherwise,[37] is seems that the metropolitan would likewise have but eight days in which to exercise his right as extraordinary collator. The starting point of this period would coincide, not with the moment when information was actually gained regarding the neglect of the diocesan chapter or body of diocesan consultors, but with the beginning of the next day. This day would constitute the first of the eight successive full days which are granted.

The extent of the extraordinary collator's power can be determined from the connotation of the term "free conferral", from the laws which pertain to that made of canonical appointment to office, and in particular from canon 158, which emphasizes the points that the extraordinary collator has but the power to confer the office, that he acquires no further right over the recipient, and that his act in no wise affects the juridical status of the recipient.[38] The right which the extraordinary collator acquires is restricted in its exercise not only by all the norms which govern the act of free conferral, but also by the general laws and particular prescripts which may affect the office in question.[39]

The Code does not in all cases say expressly that the ordinary collator or body of electors loses its rights when the *ius devolutum* becomes operative for the extraordinary collator. Hence Coronata [40] and Cheoldi (1880-1922)[41] make allowance for cases in which a concurrent jurisdiction may exist. They state that with the consent of the extraordinary collator the ordinary collator may still be permitted to use his power even after the *ius devolutivum* has become operative. They do not adduce any juridical reasons in support of this opinion,

---

[37] *Institutiones,* I, n. 594, D.

[38] "Qui alius negligentiam vel impotentiam supplens, officium confert, nullam inde potestatem acquirit in nominatum; sed huius iuridicus status perinde constituitur, ac si provisio ad ordinariam iuris normam peracta fuisset."

[39] "Provisio canonica devolvitur ad Superiorem, nisi Romanum Pontificem excipere voluerit, cum iisdem conditionibus servandis, quae pro prima provisione in iure communi vel particulari praescriptae essent."—Maroto, *Institutiones,* I, n. 587, E. c.

[40] *Institutiones,* I, n. 208, 3°, c.

[41] *Ius de Personis,* n. 134, p. 229 ,nota 4.

however, and certainly it has no foundation in pre-Code law.[42] It seems better to hold with Vermeersch (1858-1936)[43] and Wernz-Vidal[44] that the higher superior's substituted authority effectively extinguishes the previous right of the ordinary collator.

---

42 Cf. c. 5, X, *de supplenda negligentia praelatorum*, I, 10; *Glossa* ad c. 4, X, *de supplenda negligentia praelatorum*, I, 10, s. v. *patientia;* Pirhing, *Ius Canonicum in Quinque Libros Decretalium Distributum* (Dillingae, 1674-1678), lib. III, tit. VIII, p. 35; Ferraris, *Prompta Bibliotheca Canonica, Iuridica, Moralis, Theologica, necnon Ascetica, Polemica, Rubricistica, Historica* (9 vols., Romae, 1885-1889), s. v. *Electio*, IV, n. 78.

43 "De tempore utili electionis faciendae,"—*Periodica* (*de Religiosis et Missionariis*, Brugis, 1905-1919; ab anno 1920, *de Re Canonica et Morali utili praesertim Religiosis et Missionariis*, Brugis, 1927-1936, et Romae, 1937 -), XIII (1924), 72.

44 *Ius Canonicum*, II, n. 170, 4.

CHAPTER VI

The Vicar General

ARTICLE I. THE VICAR GENERAL AND THE SPECIAL MANDATE

. . . *hac potestate (providendi officiis ecclesiasticis) tamen caret Vicarius Generalis sine mandato speciali.*—Can. 152.

The vicar general is a local Ordinary,[1] but by this special provision of law he lacks power to confer ecclesiastical offices, unless he be given a special mandate to do so. The wording of this canon may have a bearing on the solution of the question whether the vicar general when authorized with a special mandate acts with ordinary or simply with delegated power, but it is not the intention of the writer to discuss this controverted point in law.

The present article will be limited to a discussion of the scope of the mandate which the bishop may give to his vicar general with respect to the conferring of offices. Augustine (1872-1943) held that, since each office is a distinct entity and each conferral a distinct juridical act, the vicar general can be given only a particular mandate for a specified act of conferral.[2] Wernz-Vidal seem to imply the same opinion when, in this connection, they state that the conferral of an office is of the character of a donation, and that the making of a donation is not authorized by means of a general mandate for free acts of administration.[3]

The major premise of these authors may be admitted, but their minor, whatever it may be, is to be denied, for their ensuing conclusion is not admissible. The wording of the canon neither indicates nor demands such a restrictive interpretation. Coronata explicitly states that this opinion of Augustine seems too severe.[4]

The majority of the authors has dealt with the question whether the bishop can by a single act of a general nature empower the vicar general to act in all those things for which the law requires that he have

---

1 Can. 198.

2 *A Commentary on the New Code,* II, 110.

3 *Ius Canonicum,* II, n. 236.

4 "Augustine requirit speciale mandatum pro singulis officiis conferendis, ita ut non valeat mandatum speciale datum pro omnibus officiis vel pro officiis determinatis. Id severius videtur nec probatur ex canone tanta severitas." —*Institutiones,* I, n. 220 § 2, p. 244, nota 3.

a special mandate, or whether the bishop needs to extend a separate specific authorization for each of the acts regarding which the various canons restrict the power of the vicar general.. Some authors hold that a single act of authorization sufficies to empower the vicar general for all these acts,[5] while other authors insist on a separate authorization for each of the various functions which postulate a special mandate.[6] Thus both groups of authors concede implicitly that the bishop can give to the vicar general a special mandate which will enable him to perform repeatedly such acts as belong to the category for which the special mandate is required. Accordingly the conferral of any and all vacant offices can be placed within the power of the vicar general by means of a single special mandate. Secondly, the conferral of offices pertains to the proper jurisdiction of the local Ordinary, which jurisdiction he can delegate in whole.[7] It is not logical that by means of a single act of delegation the bishop can give to his delegate a wider authority than he can give by means of a single special mandate to his vicar general. And, thirdly, an argument may be drawn from the general diocesan practice. It is usual, in fact it is almost a necessity, for bishops to leave general powers for conferring offices, at least those of parochial administrators, substitutes, etc., in the hands of their vicars general during the periods of their vacations and *ad limina* visits. In the light of these arguments it appears necessary to accept the conclusion that the vicar general may receive a mandate which empowers him for the execution not only of one or the other act essential for the conferral of an individual office, or of the full conferral of that office, but also of the repeated conferral of a certain type of office, or of the conferral of any and all offices in the diocese.

ARTICLE II. THE VICAR GENERAL
Sede Impedita

The vicar general assumes a peculiar position with respect to a diocese the government of which the bishop is prevented from exercising

---

5 E. g., Campagna, *Il Vicario Generale del Vescovo,* The Catholic University of America Canon Law Studies, n. 66 (Washington, D. C.: The Catholic University of America, 1931), p. 131; Vermeersch-Creusen, *Epitome,* I, n. 438; Cappello, *Summa Iuris Canonici,* I, n. 397.

6 Badii, *Institutiones Iuris Canonici in usum Scholarum* (3. ed., 2 vols., Florentiae: Libreria Editrice Fiorentina, 1921-1922), I, n. 242, d, IV; D'Angelo, *La Curia Diocesana a norma del Codice di Diritto Canonico* (Giarre [Sicilia]: Lisi, 1922), Sezione I, cap. I, n. III, pp. 16-17.

7 Can. 199, § 1.

(*sede impedita*). A bishop becomes physically impeded when one of the following causes prevents him from ruling his diocese and communicating even by letter with his subjects: captivity, whether in the hands of pagans, of heretics, of schismatics, of external enemies, or of internal foes and fellow citizens; relegation or exclusion from the diocese, exile, or inability, whether it be due to bodily or mental infirmity, cupable or inculpable.[8] In these cases the government of the diocese is in the hands of the appointed vicar general, unless the bishop or the Holy See has provided otherwise.[9] The extent of the vicar general's powers over the conferral of offices in these circumstances can be determined only by a solution of the controversy whether he governs with the restrictions placed by the Code on the power of the vicar general, or whether he governs with the powers of a vicar capitular.

Castillo, without going into detail, stated in his dissertation that *sede impedita* the bishop governs the diocese through his vicar general, in the meanwhile reserving to himself, if he wishes, the matters of graver import.[10] Campagna holds explicitly that the vicar general who governs *sede impedita* has only the ordinary power of a vicar general. He adds that the bishop could usually give a special mandate for the execution of all things which are by law withdrawn from the power of the vicar general, thus making his power equivalent to that of a vicar capitular.[11]

Both of these authors seem to have missed the whole force of canon 429, § 1. It is the very fact that the bishop cannot communicate with his subjects for the purpose of disposing of the more important matters or of granting mandates that necessitates a vice gerent. True, it could happen in some instances that he would foresee his captivity or exile, and hence would have time in which to grant a special mandate for all possible contingencies, but he could hardly foresee the more common impedients such as sickness and accidents.

Campagna gives two more reasons for his position, namely, that the

---

[8] Can. 429, § 1; cf. also, Ayrinhac, *Constitution of the Church*, p. 268.

[9] "Sede per Episcopi captivitatem, relegationem, exsilium, aut inhabilitatem ita impedita, ut ne per litteras quidem cum dioecesanis communicare ipse possit, dioecesis regimen, nisi Sancta Sedes aliter providerit, penes Episcopi Vicarium Generalem vel alium virum ecclesiasticum ab Episcopo delegatum esto."—Can. 429, § 1.

[10] *Disertacion Historico-Canonica sobre la Potestad del Cabildo en Sede Vacante o Impedida del Vicario Capitular*, p. 35.

[11] *Il Vicario Generale del Vescovo*, p. 151.

wording of canon 429, § 1, does not give the vicar general the powers of a vicar capitular, and that canon 455, § 3, confers on the vicar general in these circumstances the only additional powers which he has.[12] But neither of these interpretations of the canons seems to be correct.

There are two canons which define the usual power of the vicar general. The one states that with ordinary power he assists the bishop in his territory,[13] the other, that in virtue of his office he has the same jurisdiction over temporal and spiritual matters that the bishop has, excepting those things which the bishop reserves to himself or for which the law requires a special mandate.[14] But canon 429, § 1, states that *sede impedita* the government (*regimen*) of the diocese is in the hands of the vicar general.[15] This is the same terminology that is used in defining the power of the vicar capitular in the same canon[16] and even of the bishop himself.[17] If the vicar general has the *regimen* of the diocese, it appears not only arbitrary but also contrary to the law itself to restrict him to the limits of his ordinary office.

The second argument is that canon 455, § 3, by granting him powers in these circumstances for which he would otherwise need a mandate, implies that these are the only additional powers he receives. Again, the wording of the canon does not justify this interpretation. The canon states that the vicar general does not have these powers except (*salvo praescripto*) in the case provided for by canon 429, § 1. It does not imply that they are the only additional powers that he has. This same canon (455. § 2) speaks of the powers of the vicar capitular in like terms, but it certainly cannot be said that these are the only powers which he has, for the Code has already posited the norm that

---

12 *Il Vicaro Generale del Vescovo*, p. 151-155.

13 "Quoties rectum dioecesis regimen id exigat, constituendus est ab Episcopo Vicàrius Generalis, qui ipsum potestate ordinaria in toto territorio adiuvet."—Can. 366, § 1.

14 "Vicario Generali, vi officii, ea competit in universa dioecesi iurisdictio in spiritualibus ac temporalibus, quae ad Episcopum iure ordinario pertinet, exceptis iis quae Episcopus sibi reservaverit, vel quae ex iure requirant speciale Episcopi mandatum."—Can. 368, § 1.

15 ". . . diocesis regimen . . . penes Episcopi Vicarium Generalem . ."

16 Can. 429, § 3.

17 Can. 334, § 2.

18 "Horum (vicarios paroeciales constituere, electionem confirmare, etc.) nihil Vicario Generali competit sine mandato speciali, salvo praescripto cit. can. 429, § 1.

the vicar capitular has all the jurisdiction of the bishop excepting only those things which are expressly forbidden him by law.[19]

There are sound reasons for holding that *sede impedita* the vicar general has the power of a vicar capitular. In the first place, if the Code did not intend to grant him more extensive powers than the ones which form the normal content of his office, it was superfluous for the Code to state that the government is in his hands, for until such time as the cathedral chapter is empowered by law to assume the government of the diocese he alone, in view of the bishop's inability to act, is competent with ordinary power to act in all matters, spiritual and temporal, which are not reserved to the bishop.[20]

Secondly, it can be assumed that the determination of the powers of a vicar capitular by the Code are the result of a careful study of the needs of a diocese which is deprived of its bishop. The measure of these powers is neither greater nor less than what is sufficient. If then the vicar general did not have the fullness of these powers *sede impedita,* the capacity of his powers would not correspond to the needs of the diocese. Campagna himself recognizes this when he mentions that the bishop could give the vicar general a mandate for all acts for which it is required, thereby making his powers to be equivalent to those of the vicar capitular.[21]

There are also arguments derivable from parallel cases in the pre-Code law and from the doctrine of the authors. For instance, in a decretal which forbade anyone other than a bishop to give permission for a candidate to receive ordination, Boniface VIII added that if the bishop was remote from his diocese the vicar general could grant such permission.[22] Wernz-Vidal, in treating of suspension *ex informata conscientia,* conclude that a vicar general needs a special mandate, unless he governs the diocese *sede impedita.*[23] They evidently, therefore, hold that the vicar general is in these circumstancs not restricted by the requirements of the special mandate. And Bastnagel states that in cases

---

[19] Can. 435, § 1.

[20] Can. 368, § 1.

[21] *Il Vicario Generale del Vescovo,* p. 151.

[22] ". . . Episcopo autem in remotis agente, ipsius in spiritualibus vicarius generalis, vel, sede vacante, capitulum, seu is, ad quem tunc temporis administratio spiritualium nascitur pertinere, dare possunt licentiam ordinandi."—C. 3, *de temporibus ordinationum et qualitate ordinandorum,* I, 9, in VI°.

[23] " . . . nisi agatur de casu quo sede impedita (cf. can. 429) regimen dioecesis tenet." —*Ius Canonicum,* VI, n. 297

where the vicar general appoints parochial adjutants and assistants *sede impedita,* no general or special mandate is required. From the context it is unmistakable that he is referring to all acts of conferral, and not merely to those enumerated in canon 455, § 2.[24]

In the light of the foregoing arguments and considerations, it is the writer's conclusion that *sede impedita* the vicar general assumes the government of the diocese with all the powers of the vicar capitular.

---

[24] *The Appointment of Parochial Adjutants and Assistants,* The Catholic University of America Canon Law Studies, n. 58 (Washington, D. C.: The Catholic University of America, 1930), p. 135.

CHAPTER VII

Time Limit and Form of Conferral

ARTICLE I. CANON 155

"Officiorum provisio cui nullus terminus fuit speciali lege praescriptus, nunquam differatur ultra sex menses utiles ab habita notitia vacationis, firmo praescripto can. 458."

This law, both in its prescript and in its terminology, is taken from the legislation of the III General Lateran Council (1179) which was held under Alexander III[1] and from the authentic interpretations of that law by Innocent III.[2] The study of this canon therefore must take into consideration the pre-Code law and authors.[3]

The time is to be computed according to the norms of the third title of the first book of the Code. The *terminus a quo* is the moment of the reception by the collator of authentic notice of the vacancy of the office. The reception of the notice of vacancy will hardly coincide with the beginning of the day[4] and hence the six months will begin to run from the following midnight.[5]

The notice of the vacancy must be authentic, not in a judicial sense, but rather as opposed to rumored or presumed. The notice of the vacancy may reach the ordinary in an informal manner, but it must be such as to furnish a certitude.[6] This knowledge must relate to the

---

1 C. 8—Mansi, XXII, 222; c. 5, X, *de concessione praebendae et ecclesiae non vacantis,* III, 8.

2 Cf. c. 3, 5, X, *de supplenda negligentia praelatorum,* I, 10.

3 Can. 6, 2°, 3°.

4 The opinion of Augustine that the beginning of the day is to be taken in a moral way so as to mean something like nine o'clock in the morning (*A Commentary on the New Code,* I, 122) is contrary to the common and universal teaching of the authors, e. g., Van Hove, *De Consuetudine-De Temporis Supputatione* (Mechliniae: Dessain, 1933), n. 313; Dube, *The General Principles For the Reckoning of Time in Canon Law,* The Catholic University of America Canon Law Studies, n. 144 (Washington, D. C.: The Catholic University of America Press, 1941), p. 219.

5 Can. 34, § 3, 3°.

6 Cf. Larraona, "De Electoribus Religiosorum,"—*Commentarium pro Religiosis* [ab anno 1935, *Commentarium pro Religiosis et Missionariis*] (Romae 1920 -), VIII (1927), 293.

vacancy of the office, and not merely to an act which initiates the vacancy which is certain to follow. For instance, a bishop who receives notice of a cleric's resignation from office is by law directed to take action within a month either by accepting or by rejecting the resignation.[7] Although the remittance of the bishop's letters which accepts the resignation constitutes an act through which the office certainly becomes vacated as long as its incumbent has not recalled his resignation, yet the office is not *de iure* vacant until the resigning cleric has received the bishop's letter which accepts the tendered resignation.[8]

The term "available time" (*tempus utile*) implies that the time which is set for the exercise or prosecution of one's right does not lapse if one is ignorant of his rights or cannot act at that time.[9] There are two well defined impediments which arrest the lapse of time, namely, ignorance and the impossibility of using one's rights.

The ignorance may relate to a fact or to the law. The available time begins with the receipt of notice of vacancy, hence only when ignorance of the fact of vacancy has given way to knowledge. Ignorance of the rights given by law is not presumed,[10] nor does the Code necessarily accept any and every kind of ignorance as cancelling an otherwise changeable lapse of time, but only such ignorance as a responsible man would be apt to have. If a person does not know what is obvious to all, he himself is held responsible for the loss of his rights.[11]

The meaning of the word impediment is very general. Accordingly it points to anything that hinders one from using one's rights. Authors generally admit that an impediment stands legitimately in one's stead even when it has arisen through one's own fault. Suspension or ex-

---

7 Can. 189, § 2.

8 Can. 190, § 2.

9 Can. 35.

10 Can. 16, § 2.

11 "Ignorantiam vero hic generatim accipimus, quae cadere possit in virum prudentem; quare, si quis quod omnibus perspectum est ignoret, sui iuris amissionem sibi imputare debet."—Toso, *Ad Codicem Iuris Canonici Commentaria Minora* (5 vols., Vol I, Tiferni Tiberini: Typographica Vinciana, 1921), I, 113 (hereafter cited as *Commentaria*).

communication could therefore constitute such an impediment.[12] In addition to such legal impediments, sickness and absence from the diocese are also admissible as arresting the lapse of available time.

Prior to the Code, upon the lapse of the six months of available time, the right of conferring the vacant office passed *ipso iure* to the hands of the extraordinary collator.[13] Moreover, once this time had elapsed, any act of conferral undertaken on the part of the ordinary collator was invalid.[14] The question now arises whether these enactments have been abrogated or whether they still retain their former force.

This *ius devolutivum* has been reiterated by the Code with respect to benefices Canon 1432 § 3, states that if an Ordinary fails to confer a benefice within six months after receipt of the notice of vacancy, the conferral devolves to the Holy See,[15] unless the Ordinary's failure to confer the benefice within the six months was due, not to negligence, but to absolute want of subjects.[16] But the Code is silent concerning the application of a *ius devolutivum* in the conferral of offices which are not also benefices.

Maroto holds that canon 155[17] points implicitly to a potential *ius devolutivum* in connection with the conferral of offices just as much as canon 1432, § 3, points to it explicitly in connection with the conferral of benefices.[18] A number of authors fail to make any dis-

---

[12] An example of this is found in a decree of Innocent III wherein it was stated that within the six months prescribed by the decretal *Nulla ecclesiastica* was not to be computed the time during which the collator was under suspension, nor the time needed for his journey to Rome, his stay there, and his return.—C. 5, X, *de concessione praebendae et ecclesiae non vacantis,* III, 8; cf. also Schmalzgrueber, lib. I, tit. X, n. 5; Vermeersch-Creusen, *Epitome,* I, n. 151; Van Hove, *De Conseutudine-De Temporis Supputatione,* n. 320.

[13] C. 2, X, *de concessione praebendae et ecclesiae non vacantis,* III, 8; Reiffenstuel, lib. III, tit. V, n. 158; Wernz, *Ius Decretalium,* II, n. 324.

[14] C. 5, X, *de supplenda negligentia praelatorum,* I, 10; cf. also *Glossa* ad c. 4, X, *de supplenda negligentia praelatorum,* I, 10, s. v. *patientia;* Pirhing, *Ius Canonicum,* lib. III, tit. VIII, n. 35, § 5.

[15] "Si Ordinarius intra semestre ab habita certa vacationis notitia beneficium non contulerit, huius collatio devolvitur ad Sedem Apostolicam, salvo praescripto can. 458."

[16] Pontifical Commission for the Authentic Interpretation of the Code, 24 November, 1920—*AAS,* XII (1920), 577; reported in Bouscaren, *The Canon Law Digest,* I, 702, under canon 1432.

[17] "Officiorum provisio cui nullus terminus fuit speciali lege praescriptus, nunquam differatur ultra sex menses utiles ab habita notitia vacationis . . ."

[18] *Institutionis,* I, n. 587, D; n. 594, D.

tinction between offices as such and offices which are also benefices in the application of the *ius devolutivum.* They make the general statement that when the Ordinary collator through fault or negligence has allowed the six months to lapse, the power of conferral passes *ipso iure* into the hands of an extraordinary collator.[19] Cocchi makes the same general assertion, but adds that the extraordinary collator is the one who is specified in each instance by law,[20] from which statement it is not clear whether he means that the *ius devolutivum* applies to all offices, or only to those offices for which the law has designated an extraordinary collator. Wernz-Vidal and Coronata made a distinction between offices as such and offices which are also benefices. Wernz-Vidal state that the *ius devolutivum* does not seem to apply to offices which are not benefices,[21] and Coronata agrees that this opinion appears to have the greater probability of correctness on its side.[22]

There is no sound reason for applying the *ius devolutivum* in connection with the conferral of offices which are not benefices. In the first place, this prescript is not mentioned in canon 155 either explicitly or implicitly, and hence must be considered as abrogated.[23] Secondly, the Code enacts the general norms for all offices in canon 155, but sanctions the *ius devolutivum,* at the same time designating the extraordinary collator, only when it deals with the subsequently mentioned types of assignment of office or with individual offices.[24] It is only when the Code treats of benefices that it renews the prescript of canon 155 and adds thereto the sanction of the *ius devolutivum.*[25] Finally, the privation of the ordinary collator's right has the nature of a penalty, for it is consequent only upon his default or neglect.[26] Therefore

19 E. g., Chelodi, *Ius de Personis,* n. 135; Cappello, *Summa Iuris Canonici,* I, n. 279.

20 "Tempore utili transacto quin provisio facta sit ob culpam aut negligentiam provisoris, electorum, patroni, ius provisionis devolvitur ad superiorem qui in singulis casibus a iure designatur."—*Commentarium,* II, n. 68, 4.

21 "In officiis, quae beneficii rationem adnexam habere non solent et pertinent ad liberam collationem, illa devolutio non videtur stricte praescripta."—*Ius Canonicum,* II, n. 222.

22 *Institutiones,* I, n. 216, p. 241, nota 5.

23 "Si qua ex ceteris disciplinaribus legibus, quae usque adhuc viguerunt, nec implicite in Codice contineatur, ea vim omnem amisisse dicenda est, . . ." —Can 6, 6°.

24 E. g., can. 161; 432, § 2.

25 Can. 1432, § 3.

26 Wernz-Vidal, *Ius Canonicum,* II, n. 22; Chelodi, *Ius de Personis,* n. 134.

this privation, which must be postulated if the *ius devolutivum* is to become operative, must be interpreted strictly and restricted in its application.[27]

The *ius devolutivum,* then, does not become operative in consequence of any neglect on the part of the ordinary collator in his duty relative to the free conferral of offices which are not at the same time benefices. The one who has the right of free conferral is bound by the law to exercise that right within an available period of six months, which begins to lapse from the time that he receives certain notice of the vacancy of the office. If he fails to do so, for whatever cause, he is not thereby deprived of his right, nor does any superior beneath the Holy See acquire any right or power. It is also worthy of note that not only is there no universally sanctioned *ius devolutivum* with respect to the assignment of non-beneficed offices when the appointment thereto is to be effected by means of an act of free conferral, but neither is there any particular *ius devolutivum* whose sanction would have to be invoked in connection with the conferring of any specifically designated office.

ARTICLE II. CANON 159

Cuiuslibet officii provisio scripto consignetur

The appointment to any office is to be made in writing. The observance of this prescript is most important for the right government of the Church, but its neglect does not make the conferral invalid.[28]

---

27 Can. 19; 2219, § § 1, 3.

28 Cf. can. 11.

CHAPTER VIII

Legislation With Respect to Particular Offices

The canons on free conferral hitherto discussed dealt with the consideration of the competent authority, and with the norms governing the exercise of his power. The subject matter of the present chapter is furnished by two canons which, while serving as guiding norms for the exercise of the collator's power, look in particular to the end and the object inherent in the offices themselves. An office is a *munus* or function, an exercise of the power of orders or of jurisdiction. The object is to provide men with the means of salvation and to govern them toward the attainment of perfect happiness. The purpose of the laws to be discussed is simply this, that in the concrete the cleric to whom this function has been entrusted may act efficaciously.

ARTICLE I. OFFICES WITH THE CARE OF SOULS (CANON 154)

Officia quae curam animarum sive in foro externo sive in interno secumferunt, clericis nondum sacerdotio initiatis conferri valide nequent.

This canon does not mean to imply that in the priesthood is to be found a power of orders and of jurisdiction which suffices for the care of souls; it merely insists that the care of souls must be entrusted to no cleric who is not a priest.

In so far as each cleric, by reason of the office he holds, enjoys a power of orders or of jurisdiction not given to the laity, to that degree the laity have the right to call upon him for the exercise of that power in their behalf.[1] The salvation of souls is the supreme law; every priest is ordained for men in the things that appertain to God, and that which is given him is not for himself, but for the salvation of those for whom it was given.[2] The care of souls is, therefore, not something annexed to an office, but is rather the reason for the existence, as well as the

[1] "Praesunt autem clerici tum ordinis ministerio tum jurisdictionis imperio, ergo laicorum jus est in Ecclesia ut sive sacramentorum ministerio sanctificentur, sive jurisdictionis imperio gubernetur."—De Camillis, *Institutiones* Juris Canonici (Vol. I, Parisiis: Vives, 1868), I, 277.

[2] ". . . ministerium fuit in Ecclesia institutum, non in commodum eius cui committitur, sed in eorum salutem pro quibus confertur."—S. C. Consist., decr. *"Maxima cura,"* 20 aug. 1910—*AAS*, II (1910), 636.

end and purpose, of all ecclesiastical offices. Properly considered, therefore, every office can be thought of as being vested with the care of souls. This care is the immediate end of some offices, the mediate end of others.

The term "care of souls", however, has not this wide application in law, but rather a technical and restricted application. The term is one of long standing. From the seventh to the twelfth century the phrase *habere curam animarum* was frequently used as a synonym for the possession of episcopal jurisdiction.[3] In the Gregorian Decretal Collection it came into prominent usage in designating a certain type of office.[4]

In his decree *Exsecrabilis,* issued at Avignon in December of 1317, John XXII made an attempt to clarify the meaning of the phrase "an office with care of souls." He defined it as denoting an office in which the care of souls is exercised not by a perpetual vicar, but by the rector or minister of the office itself, that is, by one who as incumbent in the office has the rights of visitation and investigation, and the further right to receive revenues, to inflict penalties, and to absolve from them.[5]

Reiffenstuel (1642-1703) listed four requisites for this type of office: 1) that it have annexed to it the power of binding and loosing in the internal forum, and that in virtue of his office the incumbent be under the necessity of administering the sacraments to the faithful who, as subjects, are to have recourse to him; 2) that there be a determined parish or place with definite limits in which the people attached to that church reside; 3) that the incumbent of the office exercise the care of souls in his own name, and 4) that he alone, to the exclusion of others, rule in his own name over the faithful committed to his care.[6]

This definition, or rather description, as well as that of other pre-Code authors placed within the sphere of offices which had the care of souls attached to them only the offices of residential bishops, of pastors, and those who had like obligations. The same conclusion can be reached from a study of the encyclicals dealing with the obligation

---

[3] Cf. Van de Kerekhove, "De Notione Iurisdictionis in Iure Romano,"—*Jus Pontificium,* XVI (1936), 49-65.

[4] Cf. c. 28, X, *de praebendis et dignitatibus,* III, 5; Conc. Lateranen., IV, c. 29—Mansi, XXII, 1015.

[5] C. un., *de praebendis et dignitatibus,* tit. III, in Extravag. Ioan. XXII.

[6] Lib. II, tit. V, n. 29

of the *Missa pro populo.*[7]

Very few of the post-Code authors discuss the connotation of the phrase, "the care of souls", in any detail. Likewise they devote but little space to the study of the application of canon 154.. The reason is patent. There is no incentive for, and practically every reason against, appointing a cleric who is not a priest to any ecclesiastical office. Moreover, if the conferral of an office on a cleric not yet ordained to the priesthood be not invalid by reason of the rule of canon 154 or of some more specific law, such a conferral is certainly subject to recission in virtue of the rule of canon 153, § 3.[8] The reason for this is that for each ecclesiastical office in the strict sense even though it has not the care of souls attached to it, the Code expressly requires that the recipient be a priest.[9] The only possible exception to which one could point would be the case of parochial adjutants and assistants. They are called on to lend their aid and help to the pastor in the care of the souls committed to his charge and the nature of their work seems implicitly to postulate the previous reception of priestly ordination on their part, in at least the vast majority of cases, if not invariably..

Insofar as the present authors discuss at all the question of what constitutes an office which is vested with the care of souls, they attach to the concept of such an office the same meaning that pre-Code authors connected with it.[10]

Thus it is a requirement for validity not only that the offices of vicars capitular or of diocesan administrators[11] and pastors[12] be conferred upon priests, but also that the same rule be observed in the conferring of the offices of vicars general, of parish vicars, administrators, and substitutes, of rectors of seminaries, and of canons penitentiary. Zaplotnik reasons that since vicars forane must exercise a

---

7 E. g., Benedictus XIV. ep. encycl. *"Cum semper oblatas,"* 19 aug. 1774—*Fontes,* n. 345; Pii IX, litt. encyl. *"Amantissimi Redemptoris,"* 3 maii 1858—*Fontes,* n. 524; cf. also Donnellan, *The Obligation of the Missa pro Populo,* The Catholic University of America Canon Law Studies, n. 155 (Washington, D. C.: The Catholic University of America Press, 1942), pp. 45-52.

8 "Cum provisus caret qualitatibus requisitis, provisio est nulla, si ita cautum sit iure communi vel particulari aut lege fundationis; secus est valida, sed per sententiam a legitimo Superiore irritari potest."

9 Can. 367, § 1; 372 § 1; 404, § 1; 423; 445; 479, § 1, 1573, § 4.

10 Osterle, *Praelectiones Iuris Canonici* (Vol. I, Romae: Collegio S. Anselmi, 1931,) I, 92; Toso, *Commentaria,* I, 123.

11 Can. 434, § 1.

12 Can. 453, § 1.

certain vigilance and surveillance over pastors, it is likewise a requirement for validity that they be priests.[13] As for the other offices, namely, those of canons, diocesan consultors, *officiales*, chancellors, and rectors of churches, it would seem that their conferral on a cleric who is not a priest would be valid, but since it is expressly required that the incumbent of each of these offices be a priest, the conferral would certainly be illicit and rescindable.[14]

Under the pre-Code law, when it was required either by a particular or by the general law that the recipient of a certain office, or of a certain type of office, be a priest, it was sufficient that the appointed cleric received ordination to the priesthood within a year after his appointment.[15] The Code, by the careful wording of canon 154, and also of canon 1474,[16] indicates a change. To receive an office which is vested with the care of souls a cleric must now have been ordained prior to the act of conferral, or at least prior to the concession of the pastoral title.

ARTICLE II. INCOMPATIBLE OFFICES (CANON 156)

A. Can. 156, § 2: *Sunt incompatibilia officia quae una simud ab eodem adimpleri nequeunt.*[17]

The first enacted prohibitions against the simultaneous holding of multiple offices are found in the Council of Chalcedon in the year 451. [18] But since at that time there was but one so-called church (*ecclesia*) in each diocese (*paroecia*), namely the bishop's, the canons of this Council pertain more to the question of incardination and excardination than to the matter of incompatibility of offices. When the rule of this same Council, namely that every cleric should be ordained for and assigned to a definite church or service, became obsolete, avarice and ambition brought about serious abuses in the shape of the holding of several ecclesiastical offices by the same person.

Legislation to remedy this unlawful practice was enacted in the III

---

13 *De Vicariis Foraneis*, p. 60.

14 Can. 153, § 3.

15 C. 5, X, *de aetate et qualitate et ordine praeficiendorum, I,* 14; Conc. Trident., sess. XXII, *de ref.*, c. 4.

16 "Si ad beneficium obtinendum susceptio alicius ordinis requiratur, beneficiarius talem ordinem ante beneficii collationem iam receperit oportet."

17 The better arrangement seems to be to treat of the nature of incompatible offices before treating of the laws which govern their conferral.

18 E. g., c. 2, C. XXI, q. 1; c. 3, C. XXI, q. 2.

General Lateran Council (1179), [19] and again in the IV General Council of the Lateran (1215). [20] But in place of the former abuse there arose during the so-called "Babylonian Captivity" of the papacy a new reprehensible practice, the *cumulatio beneficiorum,* which flourished to a considerable degree until the time when the Council of Trent (1545-1563) enacted wholesome reform laws and subsequent Pontiffs energetically sought to enforce them. [21] The purpose which inspired the prohibition of the holding of two or more offices or benefices was twofold: to counteract avarice and ambition, and to provide for efficacious and worthy ministers. [22]

The legislation of the Council of Trent was in large part a summing up and a reiteration of the multiple decrees and enactments which, beginning with St. Gregory the Great (590-604), [23] occupied more and more space in the authentic collections of law. In general, the four following considerations were acknowledged as giving rise to incompatibility in the holding of multiple offices or benefices:

a) The consideration of the proper care of souls. Any cleric, secular or religious, if he possessed an office to which was attached the care of souls, could not validly receive another office to which was likewise attached the care of souls. [24]

b) The demand of residence. It followed from the nature of the obligations attached that an office which was vested with the care of souls implied also the obligation of residence. However, there could be, and there were, offices which did not have attached to them the care of souls, but which nevertheless required the residence of the

---

[19] C. 13—Mansi, XXII, 225; c. 3, X, *de clericis non residentibus in ecclesia vel praebenda, III,* 4.

[20] C. 13, 29—Mansi, XXII, 1002, 1015; c. 28, X, *de praebendis et dignitatibus,* III, 5; c. 9, X, *de religiosis domibus, ut episcopi sint subiectae,* III, 36.

[21] Benedictus XIV, *De Synodo Dioecesana* (2. ed., 2 vols., Mechliniae, 1842), lib. XIII, cap. VIII, nn. 1-5.

[22] Augustine, *A Commentary on the New Code,* II, 113.

[23] "Singula ecclesiastici iuris officia singulis quibusque personis singulatim committi iubemus."—Migne, *Patrologiae Cursus Completus, Series Latina,* (221 vols., Parisiis, 1844), LXXV, 110; (The decretal from which Gratian took this excerpt [c. 1, D. LXXXIX] has been preserved only in John the Deacon's life of St. Gregory.)

[24] C. 28, X, *de praebendis et dignitatibus,* III, 5; c. 9, X, *de religiosis domibus, ut episcopi sint subiectae,* III, 36; c. un., *de praebendis et dignitatibus,* tit. III, in Extravag. Ioan. XXII; Conc. Trident., sess. VII, *de ref.,* c. 5; sess. XXIV, *de ref.,* c. 17.

incumbent. The holding of such an office was also incompatible with the holding of any other residential office or benefice. [25]

c) The full assurance of sufficient sustenance. A cleric who possessed a benefice whose revenues were sufficient to support him in his proper state and condition of life could not receive another benefice. [26]

d) The prescription of a particular law or statute. In the course of time numerous cases of incompatibility with respect to particular offices were submitted to the Holy See for adjudication. From a number of decisions in such cases the principle was formulated that like offices in one church (*sub eodem tectu*) were incompatible. [27]

Only one of these considerations of incompatibility has been retained in its original terminology and connotation by the Code, and that in canon 1439, § 2, which designates as incompatible any two benefices if either of them is sufficient for the proper support of the incumbent. [28] Strictly understood, this was the only law that pertained to benefices as such. All other enactments prescinded from the question whether an office was also a benefice, and these have now been summarized in canon 156, § 2. This canon, when compared with the precepts of the old law, evidences the progress made in the science of law. The law now employs a basic precept rather than a collection of specific and concrete determinations thereof. This one and sole precept embodies the full intention of the former legislators, yet it has the flexibility of adaptation which is so essential for equity in human legislation.

Canon 156 § 2, declares that two or more offices are incompatible when the obligations inherent in these offices cannot be fulfilled by the same person at one and the same time. The extent to which this norm prserves the former provisions is evident. If the incumbent of an office has the obligation of residence as demanded by general or particular law, or as postulated by the nature of the office, he cannot possess at the same time another office which imposes the same obligation. Similarly, if the care of souls which is attached to an of-

---

[25] C. 3, X, *de clericis non residentibus in ecclesia vel praebenda*, III, 4.

[26] C. 1, X, *de excessibus praelatorum et subditorum*, V, 31; c. 19, *de praebendis et dignitatibus*, III, 4, in VI°; Conc. Trident., sess. VII, *de ref.*, c. 4; sess. XXIV, *de ref.*, c. 17

[27] Cf. c. 28, X, *de praebendis et dignitatibus*, III, 5; c. 9, X, *de concessione praebendae et ecclesiae non vacantis*, III, 8.

[28] "Incompatibilia sunt . . . duo beneficia quorum alterutrum ad honestam ipsius sustentationem sufficiat."

fice fully engages the capabilities of the incumbent, he cannot expect, or be expected, to assume added responsibilities. No one is, or can be, obliged to the impossible. In such cases the offices would be naturally incompatible by reason of the physical limitations of man.

There are also juridically incompatible offices, namely, the ones which are specified as such in the Code. For instance, the offices of vicar general and canon penitentiary are juridically incompatible, as are also those of vicar general and pastor, at least apart from a case of necessity. [29] The two categories of naturally and juridically incompatible offices are not mutually exclusive, for in most cases such offices as those of pastors are naturally as well as juridically incompatible. [30]

Even the canons which have been cited in connection with the two examples furnished preserve the flexibility of canon 156. When declaring that one person should not be both pastor and vicar general, the Code realizes that while usually these two offices are naturally incompatible, it can happen in certain cases that the obligations of a vicar general are so few, and his duties in a given parish so light, that the two offices can fall within the capabilities of a single incumbent. In such a case necessity will place an end to the juridical incompatibility. [31] But necessity, no matter how great, will never justify the uniting of the obligations of two offices in one man if he can not substantially fulfill them. Such an act would be an injustice to the recipient, to the people of the parish, and to the diocese. In like manner the Code recognizes that parishes can decrease in the number of souls to the extent that one pastor may be able to serve the people of two parishes. In such an event the Code provides for the uniting of the two parishes in one or the other admissable form, in accord with the particular exigencies or derivable advantages which attend the case. [32]

Canon 1439, § 2, intends apparently to repeat the prescript of

---

[29] "Vicarii Generalis munus ne committatur canonico poenitentiario, . . . aut, exclusa necessitate, parocho ceterisque curam animarum habentibus; . ." Can. 367, § 3.

[30] "Parochus ad norman can. 156 unam tantum titulo paroeciam habeat, nisi de paroeciis agatur aeque principaliter unitis."—Can. 460, § 1.

[31] Can. 367, § 3.

[32] "Ordinarii locorum . . . possunt, ob Ecclesiae necessitatem vel magnam et evidentem utilitatem, aeque aut minus principaliter unire quaslibet paroeci ales ecclesias inter se .. . ."—Can. 1423, § 1.

canon 156, § 2, in relation to incompatible benefices. In so doing it uses words which furnish an important clew for a fuller understanding of the law, even as applicable to non-beneficed ecclesiastical offices. [33] These words are "*onera universa*" and "*per se.*" Maroto [34] and Toso [35] stress the factor which relates to the complete fulfillment of all the obligations; Coronata [36] and Lo Gasso [37] call special attention to the factor which precludes the fullfillment of the obligations through a vicar or a delegate. Accordingly the incumbent of an office who finds it necessary to exercise that office in whole or in part through a vicar cannot take upon himself any other office the duties of which conflict with the duties of the office already possessed; nor can he possess two offices if it is necessary to exercise either of them with the assistance of a vicar or a delegate.

An exception is to be made for certain types of offices because of their temporary nature. Such offices as those of vicar capitular and diocesan administrator would not be incompatible with the office of pastor. [38] In fact, when a parish in which there are no parcchial assistants becomes vacant, the Code makes express provision for the neighboring pastor to assume the care of that vacant parish until an administrator is appointed. [39]

In practice there will, of course, arise occasions when the natural incompatibility of offices will be in doubt. A cleric may be able to fulfill to a greater or less extent the obligations of two offices, but in view of the fact that the fulfillment of the obligations is constituted as a matter of justice, and that the Code has attached certain effects and penalties to the acceptance and holding of incompatible offices, [40] there must be some ecclesiastical authority competent to give a decision. The Code, as was mentioned, does make certain determinations, but other than in these cases the judge of the compatibility of offices, is, quite logically, the ordinary collator himself. [41]

[33] "Incompatibilia sunt non solum duo beneficia, quorum onera universa idem beneficiarius per se implere simul nequeat, . . ."

[34] *Institutiones,* I, n. 595, A.

[35] *Commentaria,* I, 125.

[36] *Institutiones,* I, n. 217.

[37] "De incompatibilitate officiorum,"—*Periodica,* XXIV (1935), 34.

[38] Maroto, *Institutiones,* I, n. 595, B; Toso, *Commentaria,* I, 125.

[39] Can. 472, 2°.

[40] Can. 188, 3°; 2396.

[41] Lo Gasso, "De incompatibilitate officiorum,"—*Periodica,* XXIV (1935), 34-36.

B. Can. 156, § 1: *Nemini conferantur duo officia incompatibilia.*

The principle stands: no cleric may be given two or more offices when he is physically or juridically incapable of fulfilling their inherent duties and obligations. [42] This prescript is properly protected by two other canons. In the first place, one who receives and takes possession of an office incompatible with an office he already possesses, *ipso facto* renounces the first office, [43] and secondly, if he presumes to retain possession of both offices, he is *ipso facto* deprived of both. [44]

Natural incompatibility, or physical incapability, is not a matter which pertains simply to the realm of human positive law. For its sanction it looks to the natural law itself, hence there can be no question of a dispensation. But juridical incapability, as such, may be the subject of the dispensatory power of the Holy See. [45]

C. Can. 156, § 3: *Firmo praescripto can.* 188, n. 3, *concessio alterius officii a Sede Apostolica facta non valet, nisi in supplici libello mentio prioris incompatibilis habeatur, aut clausula derogatoria adiiciatur.*

Ordinarily, in view of his proximity to the factors present in a case, a bishop or any other local Ordinary will have more detailed knowledge than the Holy See of those things which render specific offices in his diocese incompatible. He has many and varied sources of knowledge of the needs of the offices, of the obligations attached thereto, and of the conditions and capabilities of the candidates. Hence he is in little if any danger of deception or of an inadvertent performance of acts which would redound to the harm of the Church or of souls. The Code therefore gives added protection to the acts of conferral on the part of the Holy See in its capacity of ordinary

[42] Cf. Raus, *Institutiones Canonicae juxta Novum Codicem Juris* (2. ed. Parisiis: Vitte, 1931), n. 72, IV.

[43] "Ob tacitam renuntiationem ab ipso iure admissam quaelibet officia vacant ipso facto et sine ulla declaratione, si clericus: . . . aliud officium ecclesiasticum cum priore incompatible acceptaverit et eiusdem pacificam possessionem obtinuerit: . . ."—Can. 188, 3°.

[44] "Clericus, qui assectus pacificam possessionem officii vel beneficii cum priore incompatibilis, prius quoque retinere praesumpserit contra praescriptum can. 156, 1439, utroque privatus ipso iure exsistat."—Can. 2396.

[45] Cf. can. 81; Wernz-Vidal, *Ius Canonicum*, II, n. 216, III.

or extraordinary collator by the sanctions of invalidity contained in canon 156, § 3.

Canon 156, § 3, first of all acknowledges and upholds the enactment of canon 188, 3°, which prescribes that if a cleric receive and take possession of an office incompatible with the one he already holds, he *ipso facto* renounces the first, and secondly states that the concession to a cleric by the Holy See of an office incompatible with the one he already possesses is invalid, unless in the petition there was mention of this office already possessed, or in the rescript, a derogatory clause. Regarding the interpretation of this law, there are three different opinions:

a) The proponents of the first opinion consider the initial phrase, namely, *firmo praescripto can.* 188, *n.* 3, as a mere reference or explanation which has no special force or consequence for, or even relationship to, the rest of the statute. As a result they can say, or at least imply, that if in the petition there is mention of the office possessed, or in the rescript there intervenes a derogatory clause, not only is the conferral of the second office valid, but the cleric then possesses both offices, even though they be incompatible. This opinion is held by Maroto, [46] Wernz-Vidal, [47] Toso, [48] Sipos [49] Cocchi, [50] Claeys Bouuaret-Simenon, [51] and apparently by Augustine. [52]

b) The second opinion states, first, that if in the petition there is mention of the first office, but no derogatory clause in the rescript, then the conferral made by the Holy See is valid, but the first office is lost in virtue of canon 188, 3°; secondly, that if in the rescript there is a derogatory clause, e. g. *ex certa scientia, de plenitudine potestatis, non obstantibus quibuscumque,* then not only is the conferral of the second office valid, but the cleric may validly and licitly retain both offices. [53]

The difference between the two opinions mentioned is this: the latter recognizes the concession of a dispensation from the laws of

[46] *Institutiones,* I, n. 595, D.

[47] *Ius Canonicum,* II, n. 216, III.

[48] *Commentaria,* I, 126.

[49] *Enchiridion,* n. 285, C.

[50] *Commentraium,* II, n. 69.

[51] *Manuale,* I, n. 316.

[52] *A Commentary on the New Code,* II, 114.

[53] Coronata, *Institutiones,* I, n. 217, 2°.

canons 156, § 1, [54] and 188, 3°, [55] only in the event that a derogatory clause has been added to the rescript; the former recognizes not only the grant of an explicit dispensation in the derogatory clause when it is added, but also the concession of an implicit dispensation from the afore mentioned laws whenever the rescript is issued in answer to a petition which contained mention of the incompatible office already held.

c) The third opinion grants the initial phrase, *firmo praescripto can.* 188, *n.* 3, full force throughout the statute, and consequently does not assume the grant of a dispensation from the prescripts of canons 156 § 1, and 188, 3°, unless in the rescript, a dispensation is expressly, or equivalently, conceded. [56] This opinion is the one preferred by the writer.

In the first place, the initial phrase of canon 156, § 3, must be given that force which its particular form calls for in all parallel places in the Code. [57] Whenever the phrases *firmo praescripto, salvo praescripto,* are used, [58] they have but one meaning, and that is that the canon in which they are used may not be allowed in any way to derogate from the canon which the phrases are meant to safeguard. Therefore canon 156, § 3, may not in any way be assumed as derogating from the force of canon 188, 3°. In other words, even though the Holy See issues to a cleric a valid rescript whereby he obtains an office incompatible with the one he already holds, the valid concession of the second office in and of itself precludes the continued possession of the first.

Secondly, the law points out a difference between acts of conferral made by the Holy See and those made by other local Ordinaries. When there is conferred on a cleric an office incompatible with the one he already holds, the conferral is valid if made by an Ordinary, invalid if made by the Holy See. Canon 156, § 3, simply states that

---

54 "Nemini conferantur duo officia incompatibilia."

55 "Ob tacitam renuntiationem ab ipso iure admissam quaelibet officia vacant ipso facto et sine ulla declaratione, si clericus: . . . aliud officium ecclesiasticum priore incompatibile acceptaverit et eiusdem pacificam possessionem obtinuerit; . . ."

56 Vermeersch-Creusen, *Epitome,* I, n. 274, 3; Blat, *Commentarium,* II, n. 98; Chelodi, *Ius de Personis,* n. 135, B; Cappello, *Summa Iuris Canonici,* I, n. 278; 2.

57 Can. 18.

58 E.g., can. 45; 132; 201, § 2; 1099, § 2; 1608; 1703.

a conferral made by the Holy See is valid only then when mention of the prior incompatible office was made in the petition, or when a derogatory clause was appended to the rescript. The canon assimilates a conferral made by the Holy See under either of these two conditions to a conferral made by any other collator, that is, it is valid. But to a valid conferral made by the Holy See, as well as one made by any other collator, the canon applies the prescript of canon 188, 3°. In both cases the conferral is valid, but also in both cases the first office of the recipient becomes *ipso facto* vacant through his tacit resignation when he takes possession of the second.

Thirdly, it cannot be conceded in accord with the first opinion that in the rescript an implicit dispensation is granted in answer to the petition which contained mention of the prior incompatible office. A rescript whereby an office is obtained is to be strictly interpreted. [59] Likewise, dispensations are to be strictly interpreted, [60] particularly those whereby a plurality of offices is obtained. [61] And if they are to be strictly interpreted, then any claim which favors the fact of their existence may be adduced with only the greatest of caution and reserve. By the same standards it seems temerarious to contend for the presence, in the general derogatory clause, of a dispensation which allows the recipient of the papal rescript to retain both offices, when even the conferral of the second office would not be valid apart from the derogatory clause contained in the rescript.

Gasparri's footnotes to canon 156, § 3, indicate a source which gave rise to a similar controversy in the old law. It was decreed that if a petitioner culpably concealed his possession of a benefice, the con-

---

[59] Can. 50. While it is true that this canon speaks of rescripts whereby benefices are obtained, yet, as was mentioned in the early chapters of this work, offices which were not benefices were unknown in the pre-Code law, and in the general norms of the First Book of the Code, many of which are taken *verbatim* from the old law, the distinction between offices and benefices has not been given any consideration.

[60] Can. 85.

[61] "Cum dispensationes sint odiosae, rescripta, quibus plura officia conceduntur, sunt strictae interpretationis."—Wernz-Vidal, *Ius Canonicum*, II, n. 216, III.

"Quomodo intelligi debeat dispensatio super pluralitate? Rescriptae seu litterae apostolicae super beneficiis ecclesiasticis obtinendis stricte interpretari debent. Dispensatio est vulnus iuris; . . . litterae tamen super obtinendis beneficiis impetratae debent cum sint ambitiosae, restringi."—Reiffenstuel, lib. III, tit. V, n. 250.

cession of a second benefice by means of a rescript from the Holy See was invalid, [62] unless the rescript were given *motu proprio.* [63] But a question arose as to the validity of such a concession even by means of rescript *motu proprio* when thereby a cleric would gain possession of incompatible benefices. Panormitanus (1385-1453) held that the intention of the Pontiff had to be clear in the case, otherwise there was no dispensation, and he cited Ioannes Andreae (1272-1348) as holding the same opinion. [64]

Vermeersch-Creusen, who are the clearest proponents of the third opinion, state that it is not the intention of the Holy See that both offices be retained. Hence, unless there be special mention of the grant of a dispensation from the rule of canon 188, 3°, the first office is lost through a tacit renunciation when possession is taken of the second. [65]

The second opinion admits the operative effect of the law of canon 188, 3°, in the instance in which a rescript is given in answer to a petition which contains mention of the prior incompatible office, but denies that the same rule still is in effect when the rescript contains a derogatory clause. This division or distinction is not justified by the wording of the canon. The two clauses, *in supplici libello mentio prioris incompatibilis habeatur,* and *clausula derogatoria adiiciatur,* are, by the disjunctive *aut,* made alternatives which in equal measure are dependent upon the conditional conjunction *nisi.*

The Holy See can, of course, attach to a rescript a derogatory clause which has a twofold effect, namely, of making valid what would otherwise have been invalid, and of dispensing from the laws enacted in canons 156, § 1, and 188, 3°. But, unless the very wording of the clause reveals clearly the intention of the Holy See to give it this two-fold effect, there must be attributed to it but the single effect which is warranted for it in accord with the law as enacted in

---

[62] C. 7, *de rescriptis,* I, 3, in VI°.

[63] C. 23, *de praebendis et dignitatibus,* III, 4, in VI°; c. 4, *de praebendis et dignitatibus,* III, 2, in Clem.

[64] *Commentaria* ad c. 8, X, *de rescriptis,* I, 3, n. 5.

[65] "Intentio tamen S. Sedis non est ut utrumque officium retineatur, ideoque, nisi de speciali dispensatione a c. 188 mentio fiat, capta pacifice possessione novi officii, prius ipso iure ex tacita renuntiatione vacat."—*Epitome,* I, n. 274, § 3.

canon 156, § 3.[66] In addition to Vermeersch-Creusen as cited above, this opinion is held by Blat,[67] Chelodi,[68] and Cappello.[69]

---

[66] A rescript given *motu proprio* is not of itself sufficient to have either of these effects. Cf. can. 46; Coronata, *Institutiones,* I, n. 217, 2; Augustine, *A Commentary on the New Code,* II, 114.

[67] *Commentarium,* II, n. 98.

[68] *Ius de Personis,* n. 135, b.

[69] *Summa Iuris Canonici,* I, n. 278, 2.

CHAPTER IX

The Recipients of Ecclesiastical Offices

ARTICLE I. CANON 153

A. Can. 153, § 1: *Ad vacans officium promovendus debet esse clericus, iis qualitatibus praeditus, quae a iure communi vel particulari aut a lege fundationis ad idem officium requiruntur.*

If, as Origen (185-254) says, he who is to be ordained to the priesthood must be known by all as more outstanding, more learned, more holy, and in every virtue more eminent than the rank and file of Christians, [1] then even more is to be demanded of him who by reason of an office is to share in the twofold power of orders and jurisdiction given by Christ to His Church. The minister of these powers is not only to be worthy of them, he must also be qualified to exercise them. Canon 153, § 1, requires that the recipient of an office be a cleric who possesses those qualities which the general or particular law, or the law of foundation, requires in him who is to receive the office.

This general norm requires that the recipient be a cleric, but from what was said in a previous chapter it is evident that this requisite is less than could be, and is elsewhere, made. In that chapter it was pointed out that for all ecclesiastical offices in the strict sense, the law either explicitly or implicitly demands that the recipient be at least a priest. Consequently the recipient is to have all of those qualities which must be found in a candidate for the priesthood.

Before any examination, however, of the positive qualities in detail, attention is to be given to those impediments which render a priest incapable of receiving offices. The first of these is an irregularity. Prior to the Code it was disputed whether one who had incurred an irregularity could validly receive an office. [2] At the present, from

---

1 *In Leviticum,* homil. VI.—*Migne, Patrologiae Cursus Completus, Series Graeca* (161 vols. Parisiis, 1856-1866), XII, 469.

2 Cf. Gasparri, *Tractatus Canonicus de Sacra Ordinatione* (2 vols., Parisiis, 1893-1894), I, n. 173; Wernz, *Ius Decretalium,* II, n. 303.

the wording of canon 991, § 3, [3] the authors conclude that while an irregularity prevents the valid reception of a benefice, [4] it only indirectly impedes the licit conferral of an office which carries with it any obligation of the exercise of orders. [5]

A second type of impediment is occasioned by the presence of an ecclesiastical penalty. In the first place, a priest becomes *ipso iure* incapable of receiving an ecclesiastical office when there is inflicted upon him, by condemnatory sentence, the censure of excommunication, [6] of personal interdict, [7] or of suspension. [8] The same is true of one who incurs, or upon whom is inflicted, that particular penalty whereby he becomes an *excommunicatus vitandus.* [9] A cleric who incurs the censure (*latae sententiae*) of excommunication, personal interdict, or suspension, is *ipso iure* no longer entitled to obtain an office. [10] Nevertheless, if an office is given to him prior to the declaratory sentence, the conferral is valid. [11] After the declaratory sentence, not only are conferrals of offices upon him invalid, but such conferrals as may have been made to him between the time of the incurring of the penalty and the time of the declaratory sentence are rescinded. [12]

Secondly, canon 2298, 5°, lists legal inability to receive any or certain offices as a vindicative penalty. [13] This penalty may be inflicted by a legitimate superior, or it may be incurred *ipso facto,* either by itself [14] or consequent upon some other penalty. [15]

---

[3] ". . . et dispensatus potest obtinere beneficia non consistorialia etiam curata . . ."

[4] Wernz-Vidal, *Ius Canonicum, II, n.* 199; Sipos, *Enchiridion,* n. 28, 5.

[5] Maroto, *Institutiones,* I, n. 592, c; Cappello, *Summa Iuris Cononici,* I, n 276, 3°, p. 353, nota 6; Chelodi, *Ius de Personis,* n. 134, b, p. 230, nota 4; Coronata, *Institutiones,* I, n. 211, A.

[6] Can. 2265, § 1, 2°, § 2.

[7] Can. 2275, 3°.

[8] Can. 2283.

[9] Can. 2265, § 1, 2°, § 2.

[10] Can. 2265, § 1 2°; 2275, 3°; 2283.

[11] Can. 2265, § 2.

[12] "Sententia declaratoria poenam ad momentum commissi delicti retrohait."—Can. 2232, § 2.

[13] "Poenae vindicativae quae clericis tantum applicantur, sunt: . . . inhabilitas ad omnes vel ad aliquot dignitates, officia, beneficia aliave munera propria clericorum; . . ."

[14] E. g., can. 2390, § 2; 2394, 1°; 2395.

[15] E. g., can. 2394, § 2; 2303, § 1.

A third type of impediment is the presence of a non-penal legal inability to receive an office or offices. For instance, a religious who has an indult of exclaustration can receive no office in his order or congregation the while he uses this indult; [16] a priest elected, nominated, or presented for a vacant diocese cannot be elected or appointed vicar capitular or diocesan administrator of that diocese. [17]

It is evident from the wording of the law in each of the examples cited that this inability is established with invalidating effect. There are other legal inabilities which render an act of conferral not invalid but illicit. For instance, a canon penitentiary, a brother or a nephew of the bishop, a pastor, and others who have the care of souls are excluded from the office of vicar general; [18] a religious who has received an indult of secularization may not receive any benefice in major or minor basilicas, or in cathedral churches, nor any office in seminaries, in colleges, in universities, in religious houses or in the episcopal curia. [19] These are but a few of the legal inabilities imposed by the Code.

Finally, in addition to these legal impediments and inabilities, there are what may be called natural impediments. For instance, a priest totally incapacitated in consequence of insanity, or sickness, or of injury, could not be given an office; partial incapacity would impede the licit conferral of office or at least of certain types of office.

For all offices, as well as for each office in particular, the Code demands certain positive qualities, in addition to which others may be required by particular law, or by the law of foundation. Requisites of particular law are the legal demands which are made with reference to a certain office, to a certain type of office, or to all offices, in a particular place, diocese, province, or nation. [20] Such a requisite is exemplified, for instance, in the statutes which require that the recipients of specified offices in certain cathedral chapters in Germany belong to a certain nation, family, or nobility. [21]

Like requirements may be found in the law of foundation. The law of foundation has a twofold meaning: a) the decree of ecclesias-

---

16 Can. 639.

17 Can. 434, § 1.

18 Can. 367, § 3.

19 Can. 642, § 1.

20 Cicognani, *Canon Law* (authorized English version, by J. O'Hara and F. Brennan, Philadelphia: Dolphin Press, 1934), p. 501.

21 Augustine, *A Commentary on the New Code,* II, 111.

tical authority whereby an office is constituted in its own juridical personality, and, b) the complexus of requisites and conditions which a founder in the act of foundation attaches to some particular office. [22] In its first meaning there could be a law of foundation with regard to an office, but in its second meaning it can have place only in the founding of a benefice. In the foundation the founder may, with the consent of legitimate authority, require qualities in the recipient not only beyond the common law, but even contrary to it, provided that they are laudable and consistent with the nature of the benefice. [23]

> B. Can. 153, § 3: *Cum provisus caret qualitatibus requisitis, provisio est nulla, si ita cautum sit iure communi vel particulari aut lege fundationis; secus est valilda, sed per sententiam a legitimo Superiore irritari potest.* [24]

It was noted in the foregoing section that the presence of certain impediments or inabilities in a candidate for office renders the act of conferral invalid, and that the presence of other disabilities renders it merely illicit. Similarly, of the positive qualities required by the common law, some are necessary for the valildity, others for the licitness of the act of conferral. The order of priesthood is required for validity in the recipients of offices to which is attached the care of souls, [25] whereas it is required but for licitness in the recipients of other ecclesiastical offices. It is also required for validity that a vicar capitular or diocesan administrator be thirty years of age. All other qualities required by the code on the part of candidates for particular offices—excepting requisites for recipients of offices in religious orders and congregations—for example, age, prudence, academic degrees, etc., [26] need be found in the recipient only for the

---

[22] Coronata, *Institutiones,* I, n. 211, 1°; Beste *Introductio,* p. 200; S. C. Conc., *Resolutio,* 10 feb. 1923—*AAS,* XV (1923), 544.

[23] Can. 1417. Cf. S. C. Conc., *Resolutio,* 10 feb. 1923—*AAS,* XV (1923), 544; reported in Bouscaren, *The Canon Law Digest,* I, 224, under can. 403.

[24] The better arrangement seems to be to treat of the legal sanctions enacted in law in connection with the conferral of offices upon unqualified candidates, and then to discuss the question of the candidates' qualifications for office.

[25] Can. 154.

[26] Cf. can. 367, § 1; 373, § 4; 396, § 3; 423, § 2; 1360, § 1; 1573, § 4.

licitness of the conferral. [27]

Canon 153, § 3, reiterates and applies the prescripts of cannon 11 by stating that when the recipient of an office lacks those qualities which are required in him for validity by general or particular law, or by the law of foundation, the act of conferral is invalid. [28] The canon then further states that if the recipient of an office lacks those qualities which are required in him only for licitness by general or particular law, or by the law of foundation, the act of conferral is valid, but may be rescinded by the sentence of a legitimate superior. There is nothing new in this particular idea. Pre-Code law also recognized that there are many prohibited acts which, once they have been placed, are nevertheless recognized as valid, [29] but which, though they have been tolerated up to the present, may not be once the demands of justice require that judgment be passed upon them. [30]

Canon 153, § 3, furthermore states that in the absence of qualities required for licitness in the recipient, the conferral may be rescinded. It is not stated that a rescission must take place. The reason for this is that a certain other quality may be present in a degree sufficient to supply for what is lacking, or there may not be a fully qualified cleric on whom to bestow the office. [31] Claeys Bouuaert-Simenon state that it is left to the prudent judgment of the superior to decide whether or not the conferral is to be rescinded. [32] From the wording of canon 1667 [33] it may seem that one who possessed the right to the exercise in his behalf of the power of orders or jurisdic-

---

[27] "Irritantes aut inhabilitantes eae tantum leges habendae sunt, quibus aut actum esse nullum aut inhabilem esse personam expresse vel aequivalenter statuitur."—Can. 11.

[28] Although it is not immediately evident from the wording of canon 153, § 3, it is to be kept in mind that its prescripts have application not only in the event of the absence of requisite qualities, but also when there is present one or the other of the legal or natural impediments or inabilities mentioned in the previous section. Cf. Coronata, *Institutiones,* I, n. 211, 1°.

[29] ". . . quia multa fieri prohibentur, quae, si facta fuerint, obtinent roboris firmitatem."—C. 16, X, *de regularibus et transeuntibus ad religionem,* III, 31.

[30] "Cum multa per patientiam tolerentur, quae, si deducta fuerint in iudicium exigente iustitia, non debent tolerari."—C. 16, X, *de praebendis et dignitatibus,* III, 5.

[31] Toso, *Commentaria,* I, 123.

[32] *Manuale Iuris Canonici,* I, n. 314, II.

[33] "Quodlibet ius non solum actione munitur, nisi aliud expresse cautum sit, sed etiam exceptione, quae semper competit et est suapte natura perpetua."

tion annexed to a certain office, thinking himself to suffer injury by reason of defect in the incumbent of that office, could institute judicial action. This, however, is excluded by a response of the Pontifical Commission for the Interpretation of the Code, May 22, 1923. It was asked:

> 1. Whether according to canons 1552-1601 a judicial action can be instituted against the decrees, acts, and dispositions of Ordinaries, which pertain to the administration of their dioceses; for example, appointments to benefices, offices, etc., or refusal to make such appointments. And if not, then,
>
> 2. Whether a judicial action can be instituted at least for damages resulting from such decrees, acts, and dispositions; so that the Ordinary can, according to can. 1557, § 2, and can. 1559, § 2, be summoned before the tribunal of the Sacred Roman Rota.

Reply: In the negative to both; *et ad mentem*: The mind is that it belongs exclusively to the Sacred Congregations to take cognizance both of such decrees, acts, and dispositions, and of the damages which may be claimed to have resulted therefrom. [34]

The judicial term *sententia*, therefore, as used in canon 153, § 3, is not to receive a strict interpretation, since in virtue of this response all judicial action, both in rescinding a valid act of conferral, and in declaring one invalid, is excluded.

C. Can. 153, § 2: *Assumatur, omnibus perpensis, magis idoneus sine ulla personarum acceptione.*

Of those qualities which fit a candidate for an office, some will be absolute, others will admit of varying degrees of perfection. For instance, age is an absolute quality, whereas the degree of learning differs in each individual. Secondly, there are qualities which may be called personal, others which will be of moment only with respect to certain offices. For instance, sanctity of life is a personal virtue, whereas linguistic ability in a priest may make him a more fit recipient of a certain office than others who lack this gift. The recipient of an office is to be that priest who not only possesses the absolute and personal qualities required by divine law, whether natural

[34] *AAS, XVI* (1924), 251; reported in Bouscaren, *The Canon Law Digest,* I, 739, under canon 1552.

or positive, and by ecclesiastical law, but who also is more fitted by reason of higher perfection in those qualities which admit of degrees of perfection, and likewise by reason of qualities relative to the peculiar needs and circumstances of the office in question. [35]

Although the authors use the terms *dignus* and *indignus* in treating of this canon, [36] the Code in this and in parallel places chooses the more flexible and more juridical expressions *idoneus* and *non idoneus*. One is fit, just as one is worthy, if he lacks none of the qualifications prescribed by law, but the more fit, though not necessarily the more worthy, candidate is he who possesses these qualifications in a more conspicuous degree. [37] Every unworthy (*indignus*) person is also unqualified (*non idoneus*), but not every unqualified person is unworthy. A particular note of moral deficiency attaches to the term "unworthy." [38]

The presence or absence of the qualities demanded by law as well as the degree of fitness of the candidate must be judged by a competent ecclesiastical authority. Sipos [39] and Augustine [40] state merely that this authority is the Ordinary, while Cocchi [41] and Moroto [42] are more explicit in stating that this authority, at least with respect to minor offices, is the Ordinary of the place to whom the incumbent of the office will be subject in the exercise of the obligations of that office, not only when this Ordinary is the collator, but also when the office is conferred by some one else. The Code leaves not only this judgment to the prudence of the superior but also, with but few exceptions, the means whereby he is to obtain the basis for it.

The exceptions come into play in the selecting of recipients of offices and parishes by means of *concursus,* and in the designating of pastors and parish vicars. A *concursus* is essentially an examina-

---

35 Can. 153, § 2. Wernz, *Ius Decretalium,* II, n. 309; Smith, *Elements of Ecclesiastical Law,* I, 161.

36 E. g., Wernz-Vidal, *Ius Canonicum,* II, n. 206; Sipos, *Enchiridion,* n. 29, § 3.

37 Augustine, *A Commentary on the New Code,* II, 111.

38 Moersdorf, *Die Rechtssprache des Codex Iuris Canonici* (Veroeffentlichungen der Goerresgesellschaft, Sektion fuer Rechts-und Staats-wissnschaft, Heft 74, Paderborn: Schoeningh, 1937), p. 35.

39 *Enchiridion,* n. 28, § 5, b.

40 *A Commentary on the New Code,* II, 112.

41 *Commentarium,* II, n. 640.

42 *Institutiones,* I, n 571, c.

tion of candidates.[43] The Code prescribes an examination of the candidates for a parish[44] and of the one presented as parish vicar.[45] No power of dispensing from the requirements of the *concursus* is given to the Ordinary, but he may in the case which is listed in canon 459, § 3, 3°, dispense from the examination of the candidate for a parish or for the office of parish vicar.[46]

There is one particular element which must be excluded from the determination of the recipient of an office. This prohibition is expressed in a phrase which is of frequent occurrence in the Code, namely, *sine ulla personarum acceptione.* The evil of favoritism is present when the recipient is chosen not because of personal merits and qualities relative to the office, but because of some extrinsic circumstances such as friendship, consanguinity, etc.[47] The conferring of an office upon a priest for such unworthy motives is an act contrary to distributive justice,[48] that is, against the constant and permanent determination of the society, functioning through its authorized officials, to give to each subject his due.[49]

If the collator confers an office upon a priest qualified for it, passing over one who is better qualified, the conferral is valid, but illicit; the act cannot be rescinded, nor is there any recourse granted to the injured party,[50] unless the determinatioon of the recipient was made by means of a *concursus.*[51]

ARTICLE II. CANON 157

"Officium vacans per renuntiationem vel per sententiam privationis nequit ab Ordinario, qui renuntiationem acceptavit aut sententiam tulit, valide conferri suis aut resignantis familiaribus, consanguineis vel affinibus usque ad secundum gradum inclusive."

If the purpose of ecclesiastical offices is to be adequately fulfilled, then worthy and capable incumbents must be selected for these of-

43 Cf. can. 399, § 2; 459, § 4; Benedictus XIV, const. *"Cum illud,"* 14 dec. 1742 — Codex I. C., Documentum IV.

44 Can. 459, § 3, 3°.

45 Can. 471, § 2.

46 "Clericum examini super doctrina coram se et examinatoribus synodalibus subiiciat; a quo, de consensu eorumdem examinatorum potest dispensare, si agatur de sacerdote doctrinae theologicae laude commendato."

47 Beste, *Introductio,* p. 201.

48 Blat, *Commentarium,* II, n. 95; Coronata, *Institutiones,* I, n. 211, 1°.

49 LeBuffe-Hayes, *Jurisprudence* (3. ed., New York: Fordham University Press, 1938), p. 217.

fices. It is this ideal that is to motivate all collators in the exercise of their power of conferral. Realizing, however, that ideals may be lost and motives become warped, the Church has tried by her legislation to direct the exercise of this power in its proper channel and to erect barriers to the entrance of harmful elements. One influence that has ever been a threat to the right order of the Church has been nepotism. The preference that every man has for those closely related to him is very natural. It is something which is rooted in nature itself. It has a peculiar quality of unselfishness which accords it an elusive part in the motivation of acts. In itself it is not wrong. But more than anything else it is the motivation in whole or in part of acts contrary to distributive justice in both the civil and ecclesiastical societies. To check its influence has ever been one of the objects of ecclesiastical legislation.

In this matter as affecting the conferral of offices the first positive step was taken by Pope Pius IV (1559-1565) in his *Motu proprio "Cupientes."* The law was directed against all possible abuse in the appointment of the collator's relatives or domestic associates to benefices which became vacant through an act of deprivation or removal on the part of the collator. The acts of all collators of offices, even if the collators were Cardinals, remained without juridical effect or validity if benefices thus made vacant were conferred by them upon their own relatives by blood or marriage, or upon clerics of their own household.[52] Eight years later Pope St. Pius V (1566-1572) amplified this law in his Constitution "*Quanta Ecclesiae.*" In virtue of this constitution a benefice resigned into the hands of the collator could not be conferred validly either upon the collator's own relatives or domestic associates, or upon the relatives or domestic associates of the cleric who resigned the office.[53]

These provisions are now substantially embodied in canon 157.[54]

---

50 Wernz-Vidal, *Ius Canonicum,* II, n. 208; Sipos, *Enchiridion,* n. 29 § 3; Chelodi, *Ius de Personis,* n. 134, c.

51 Benedictus XIV, const. "*Cum illud,*" 14 dec. 1742, § 1—Codex I. C. Documentum IV.

52 11 oct. 1560, § 1 — *Fontes,* n. 99.

53 1 apr. 1568, § 5 — *Fontes,* n. 125.

54 "Officium vacans per renuntiationem vel per sententiam privationis nequit ab Ordinario, qui renuntiationem acceptavit aut sententiam tulit, valide conferri suis aut resignantis familiaribus, consanguineis vel affinibus usque ad secundum gradum inclusive."

Moreover this canon contains a determination not found in the former legislation. The law now specifies exactly the degrees within which it bars relatives by blood or by marriage from being validly appointed to vacant offices. Under the present law only those who are related within the second degree inclusive are excluded.

The law is directed to all Ordinaries in their capacity of collators of the offices which have become vacant through an act of resignation on the part of the incumbent, or in consequence of a sentence of deprivation. But the law becomes applicable only when these same Ordinaries have received the resignation or passed the sentence of deprivation. The law has no application when, in consequence of a canonical election, nomination, or presentation, clerical relatives or household members have gained a *ius ad rem* with reference to the offices made vacant through the incumbent's resignation or deprivation. In such circumstances, provided only that the candidate has the proper fitness for the office, the Ordinary has the obligation to confirm the elected candidates,[55] and to institute in office the one who has been presented as a fit candidate [56] or the one who has been nominated for the office.[57] But when the recipient of the office is determined by means of a *concursus,* then the Ordinary is barred from appointing his clerical relatives or household members to offices which became vacant in consequence of his previous acceptance of the resignation or as a result of his sentence of deprivation.[58]

Ordinarily it will be easy to determine both the Ordinary to whom pertains the right of deprivation or the right of accepting the resignation, and also the Ordinary who has the right of conferring the office. But a difficulty seems to arise in connection with a case in which the *officialis* or the diocesan tribunal has a part in passing the sentence of deprivation of office, or in which the vicar general, acting in virtue of a special mandate, has a part in accepting the resignation or in making the conferral. The bishop, the vicar general, the *officialis,* and the diocesan tribunal constitute one legal entity. Yet their acts are naturally distinct, and the motives behind their acts are

55 Can. 177 § 2.

56 Can. 1466, § 1.

57 Can. 471, § 2.

58 Benedictus XIV, *De Synodo Dioecesana,* lib. XIII, cap. XXIV, nn. 3-4; Santi, *Praelectiones Juris Canonici* (2. ed., 5 vols, in 2, Ratisbonae: Pustet, 1886), lib. I, tit. IX, n. 21; Ferraris, *Bibliotheca,* s.v. "resignation," n. 43.

proper to the individuals. It is not the motives of the bishop that impel a tribunal to pass a sentence of deprivation; it is not the motives of the bishop that impel a vicar general to accept a resignation when he acts in virtue of a special mandate.

Now, since the text of the law leaves obscure its application in the event that the acts are placed by the vicar general, by the *officialis*, or by the diocesan tribunal, it follows that in the absence of parallel passages in the Code the interpretation of the law must be based upon the purpose of the law and the intention of the legislator.[59] And, further, it must be kept in mind at the same time that the law in question is of a character which restricts the free exercise of a general right. Therefore a strict interpretation, that is, one which will respect the general right as much as the wording of the restrictive law allows, is here indicated.[60]

The purpose of the law, as expressly stated in the above mentioned *Motu proprio* and Constitution, and as patent from the law itself, is to obviate every semblance of simony and particularly the possibility of nepotism. Accordingly, considering first the possible acts of the vicar general in receiving resignations or in conferring offices, and secondly the possible acts of an *officialis* or of a tribunal in passing sentence of deprivation, one may list the following applications of the law as suited to the achievement of its purpose.

a) When a bishop receives a resignation, and thereupon exercises his power of conferral over the office thus made vacant, his clerical relatives and domestic associates, but not those of his vicar general, are excluded from receiving appointment to the office.[61]

b) When a vicar general receives a resignation and/or has the power of conferral over the office thus vacant in virtue of a mandate which gives him no discretionary power, it is the bishop's relatives and domestic associates who are excluded, not his own. The reason for this is that when a vicar general acts in virtue of a mandate which leaves him no discretionary powers his sole motive is his obedience to the bishop. It is possible for the motive of nepotism to enter in the motives of the grantor, but not into those of the executor.

---

59 Can. 18.

60 Can. 19.

61 Reiffenstuel, lib. I, tit. IX, n. 117; Ferraris, *Bibliotheca,* s.v. "resignatio," n. 43; Coronata, *Institutiones,* I, n. 220, § 2.

c) When a vicar general receives a resignation and has the power of conferral in virtue of a special mandate which leaves him full discretionary powers, it is his relatives, not those of the bishop, who are excluded.

d) When the vicar general has discretionary powers through a special mandate for receiving the resignation, while his superior retains and exercises the faculty of choosing the next incumbent, or vice versa, the relatives and domestic associates of neither are excluded. It is true that the two acts are in the hands of two persons who constitute but one jurisdictional Ordinary, yet to exclude the relatives and domestic associates of either person, or of both, would be to impose a restriction not intended by the law.[62]

Deprivation of office is an ecclesiastical penalty which may, or in cases must, be inflicted by a judge or tribunal as punishment for certain crimes. Just as the vicar general constitutes one person with the bishop in the exercise of voluntary jurisdiction, so also the *officialis* and the diocesan tribunal constitute one person with the bishop in the exercise of judicial power.[63] But the same latitude of interpretation which was given in the event of a resignation and a subsequent conferral cannot be given in the event of a deprivation of office by an *officialis* or a tribunal and a subsequent conferral by the bishop. The reason is to be found in the direct intervention which the bishop must exercise for the initiation of these cases.

In the first place, it is the bishop to whom the denunciation of the crime is referred,[64] and who, unless the crime be notorious or entirely certain, decides whether or not there shall be an investigation.[65] Again, it is the bishop who carries out the investigation or appoints a delegate for that purpose.[66] And finally, it is the bishop who gives a special mandate to the *officialis* to pass judgment on the results of the investigation, or who passes judgment personally,[67]

---

[62] "Diximus potiori iure affirmandum erit, cum pro iis stat regula, quae docet Pianam constitutionem locum non habere in iis beneficis quae licet in manibus Episcopi resignentur, eorum tamen collatio spectat non ad ipsum Episcopum sed ad alium." — Benedictus XIV, *De Synodo Dioecesana*, lib. XIII, cap. XXIV, n. 7.

[63] Can. 1572, § 1.

[64] Can. 1936.

[65] Can. 1942, § 2.

[66] Can. 1940.

[67] Can. 1946, § 1.

who decides whether a judicial reproof is sufficient and, lastly, who grants the special mandate to the promotor of justice for the institution of the trial.[68] Hence, while the actual sentence of deprivation may be beyond the influence of nepotism on the part of the bishop, there is too much opportunity for it in the acts preliminary to the trial for a distinction to be made between the bishop judging *per se* and the bishop judging *per alium*. Consequently, whether the Ordinary passed the sentence of deprivation *per* se or *per alium*, his relatives and household members are excluded from receiving the office thus made vacant.

Another question centers in the connotation of the terms used. Canon 157 speaks of the two canonical acts—the resignation and the sentence of deprivation—without any further specification, but both the wording and the intent of the law indicate certain restrictions.

A few authors state that not only the act of express resignation but also the act of tact renunciation as mentioned in canon 188 is contemplated in the text of canon 157.[69] To admit that all-inclusive force for the text of this canon seems unwarranted. The purpose of the law is to eliminate any and every potential desire of an Ordinary to obtain an office for his relative or domestic associate as a motive for his acceptance of a resignation from the office. Now, since in the instances enumerated in canon 188 the law itself sanctions the resignation, there can be no question of a motive on the part of any Ordinary for an acceptance of the resignation. Secondly, the acts listed in canon 188 as the effective sources of resignation are of such grave import that it is at least improbable that a cleric would execute any of them with the hope or expectation that one of his own relatives should receive the office thus vacated. Finally, the law in canon 157 is explicitly worded in such a manner that it postulates on the part of the Ordinary not one but two distinct acts in relation to the same office, namely, his acceptance of the resignation from the office and his appointment to the same office by way of an act of free conferral.

As for deprivation of office, that penalty may be inflicted either *ipso iure*, or by an act of a legitimate superior.[70] Canon 157 uses the words *qui sententiam privationis tulit,* which clause seems to

---

[68] Can. 1954.

[69] Coronata, *Institutiones,* I, n. 220, 2°; Toso, *Commentaria,* I, 126.

[70] Can. 192, § 1.

point to a condemnatory sentence which effects the deprivation rather than to a declaratory sentence which merely confirms it. When deprivation is incurred *ipso iure* the office is vacant prior to the declaratory sentence, which has but the effect of making a penalty for a delict that was not notorious enforceable in the external forum.[71]

The present law, then, is applicable only in the event of a *ferendae sententiae* penalty.[72]

In addition to the vindicative *ferendae senteniae* penalties of deprivation[73] which are ordinarily inflicted by means of a judicial process, there are deprivations of office which are inflicted by means of the administrative process which is intimated in canon 192, § 3, and outlined in titles XXVII, XXVIII, XXX, XXXI, XXXII, of the Fourth Book of the Code. If the Ordinary has decreed, *per se* or *per alios*,[74] a deprivation of office either in a judicial or in an administrative process, then, in virtue of canon 157, his relatives and domestic associates become ineligible for the office which has thus become vacant.[75] It should be noted, however, that this law does not have application in the event of the transfer of a pastor from one parish to another by means of the administrative procedure outlined in canons 2162-2167.[76]

There is little if any difficulty in determining which relatives by blood or by marriage become ineligible as prospective recipients of the vacant office in consequence of the particular degree of their relationship, for the rules of computation are clearly given in canons 96 and 97. But the proper determination of him who is domestic associate is not free of all difficulty. The term *familiaritas* was used by the Council of Trent to designate a title by means of which a bishop could become the proper bishop for the ordination of a cleric.[77] Both this Council and the Constitution "*Speculatores*" of Innocent

---

[71] Cf. can. 2232, § 1.

[72] Toso, *Commentaria*, I, 126.

[73] Cf. can. 2298, 6°.

[74] "In unaquaque dioecesi et pro omnibus causis a iure expresse non exceptis, iudex primae instantiae est loci Ordinarius, qui iudiciariam potestatem exercere potest iuse per se vel per alios, secundunt tamen canones qui sequuntur." — Can. 1572, § 1.

[75] Coronata, *Institutiones*, I, n. 220, 2°; Toso, *Commentaria*, I, 126.

[76] Cappello, *Summa Iuris Canonici*, I, n. 281, p. 344, nota 3; cf. Benedictus XIV, *De Synodo Dioecesana* ,lib. XIII ,cap. XXIV, n. VIII.

[77] Sess XXIII, *de ref.*, c. 9.

XII (1691-1700)[78] postulated for the validity of this title a service in the episcopal residence and support by the bishop for a period of three years.

The authors all list two requisites essential for the concept of *familiares,* namely, residence in the house of, and a relationship of dependence upon, him who in Roman Law terminology holds the place of the *paterfamilias.*[79] This dependence relates particularly to the matter of sustenance and the element of service.[80] Claeys Bouuaert-Simenon hold that three years of residence and dependence are necessary to establish the relatinship of *familiaritas,*[81] but Osterle considers this opinion to be wrong. He reasons, first, that the Council of Trent and the Constitution of Innocent XII required a three-year period of *familiaritas* as a title for ordination, but that the relationship itself began with the inception of residence and dependence; and that, secondly, although the Code has omitted mention of *familiaritas* as a title for ordination, it uses the term in canon 328 in relation to the *familiares* of the Holy Father, from which canon it is evident that the relationship exists for the *familiares* from the moment they are received into the papal family or household.[82]

Practically considered according to the usual arrangement as found in this country, about the only case of a domestic associate of the bishop will be that of the bishop's personal secretary.[83] It may well be that the vicar general or the chancellor have residence with the bishop and eat at table with him, but such officials are not the personal servants of the bishop, but the public servants of the diocese, and it is from the diocese that they receive their support. For the same reason a parochial assistant does not contract the relationship of *familiaritas* with his pastor.

There are but two additional points to be noted in connection with canon 157. The first is that an Ordinary is not forbidden to confer

---

[78] 4 nov. 1694 — *Fontes,* n. 258.

[79] Sipos, *Enchiridion,* n. 29, § 3; Cocchi, *Commentarium,* II, n. 70; Vermeersch, "Familiares in genere et in Codice," — *Periodica,* XIX (1930), 63-67.

[80] Cf. can. 1221, § 3; c. 5, *de verborum significatione,* V, 12, in VI°; Vermeersch, "De vera familiaritatis ratione et de familiaribus," — *Periodica,* III (1914), 85.

[81] *Manuale Iuris Canonici,* I, n. 317.

[82] *Praelectiones Iuris Canonici,* I, 92.

[83] Cf. Vermeersch, "Familiares in genere et in Codice," — *Periodica,* XIX (1930), 64.

an office on his own relative or domestic associate when the resignation was acepted, or when the sentence of deprivation was passed, by that Ordinary's predecessor. In that instance, the whole *ratio* of the law ceases.[84] The second is that the relatives and domestic associates of the one who was deprived of an office are not barred from receiving that office, for the canon speaks only of the relatives and domestic associates of the one who has resigned his office.[85]

[84] Coronata, *Institutiones,* I, n. 220, 2°.
[85] Maroto, *Institutiones,* I, n. 589, E, V, 3°.

CONCLUSIONS

1. Free Conferral (*libera collatio*) is the form of canonical assignment of office which is most in accord with the dogmatic and juridic principles of the constitution of the Church; all sanctioned rights of election, presentation, and nomination are in existence only insofar as they have been legitimately acquired from the Supreme Pontiff and residential bishops through the meditation of law, custom, or prescription.

2. It can be demonstrated definitely that the conferring of an office is an act of voluntary jurisdiction.

3. The better opinion contends that the concept of an ecclesiastical office in the strict sense postulates an ordinary power of jurisdiction.

4. The following offices in a diocese are offices in the strict sense: the offices of the canons of cathedral and collegiate chapters, of the vicar general, of the diocesan consultors, of the *officialis*, of the *vice-officialis*, of the chancellor, of the vicars forane, of the pastors, of the parish vicars, of the parochial administrators and substitutes, and of the rectors of churches and of seminaries. To the offices of parochial adjutants and assistants the law attaches a character which is so elastic in its potential concept that it precludes an exact determination of their nature in the abstract.

5. With the exception of parishes and perpetual benefices, a vicar capitular, or a diocesan administrator, has the full and free right of conferral of all offices in a diocese.

6. The metropolitan or senior suffragen upon whom devolves the right and duty of appointing a vicar capitular when the cathedral chapter has failed to do so within eight days after notice of the vacancy of the diocese has but eight days within which to fulfill his office.

7. A vicar general may receive a special mandate for one or for all the essential acts of conferral, for the conferral of an individual office, for the conferral of a certain type of office, or for the conferral of all offices in the diocese.

8. The vicar general who assumes the government of the diocese *sede impedita* has all the rights and duties of a vicar capitular.

9. The *ius devolutivum* which became operative upon the ordinary collator's failure to fill an office within the specified lapse of

time, or in consequence of his non-observance of the requisite form of conferral, or also in view of the unworthiness of the appointed recipient of office, was applicable to all offices before the enactment of the present Code. It still is applicable to certain types of office under specified conditions, e. g., to the office of pastor. But it no longer has any application to those offices which by law are subject to the full and free right of conferral at the hands of an ordinary collator.

10. When an extraordinary collator is called upon to act by reason of the *ius devolutivum,* then the right of this superior effectively extinguishes the right of the inferior. Hence an act of conferral made by the ordinary collator, or an election performed by a body of electors, after the *ius devolutivum* has become operative is devoid of all juridical validity.

11. If a cleric possesses two offices, either of which he finds necessary to exercise in whole or in part through a delegate or an assistant he is in possession of naturally incompatible offices, and therefore on the date on which he took possession of the second office the first became vacant. An exception, however, is to be made for the holding of offices whose duties do not conflict, for example, a cleric may hold both the office of pastor and the office of diocesan consultor or vicar forane.

12. Neither the rule of canon 156, § 3, nor the derogatory clause mentioned therein implies the concession of a dispensation from the law of canon 188, 3°; wherefore, when the Holy See confers upon a cleric an office incompatible with the one he already possesses, the conferral is valid if in the petition mention was made of the prior office, or if in the rescripti there is a derogatory clause, but the cleric loses possession of the first office when he takes possession of the second.

13. All ecclesiastical offices have annexed to them the care of souls either directly or indirectly, but in using the phrase "offices vested with the care of souls" the Code points only to the offices of local Ordinaries, vicars forane, pastors, parish vicars, parochial administrators and substitutes, rectors of seminaries, and canons penitentiary.

14. The purpose of canon 157 demands in some cases, permits in others, that, insofar as the disqualfiying effects of the law are con-

cerned, the bishop and his vicar general acting in virtue of a special mandate which gives him full discretionary powers be considered two distinct Ordinaries. However, in the case of a deprivation of office which is inflicted by a tribunal or by an *officialis* as a penalty for a crime, the clerical relatives and domestic associates of the local Ordinary are excluded from receiving the office thus made vacant.

15. An Ordinary may confer an office which has become vacant through a tacit resignation upon his own relatives and domestic associates as well as upon those of the former incumbent of the office.

BIBLIOGRAPHY

Sources

Acta Apostolicae Sedis, Commentarium Officiale, Romae, 1909-

Acta et Decreta Concilii Plenarii Baltimorensis III, A. D., MDCCCLXXXIV, Baltimorae, 1886.

Bouscaren, T. Lincoln *The Canon Law Digest,* 2 vols., Milwaukee: Bruce, 1934-1943.

Canones et Decreta Sacrosanctae Oecumenici Concilii Tridentini, Taurini, 1913.

Codex Iuris Canonici Pii X Pontificis Maximi iussu digestus Benedicti Papae XV auctoritate promulgatus, Romae: Typis Polyglottis Vaticanis, 1917.

Codicis Iuris Canonici Fontes cura Emi Petri Card. Gasparri editi, 9 vols., Romae (postea Civitate Vaticana): Typis Polyglottis Vaticanis, 1923-1939 (Vols. VII-IX ed. *cura et studio Emi Iustiniani Card. Serédi*).

Concilii Plenarii Baltimorensis II, in Ecclesia Metropolitana Baltimorensi, a die VII. ad diem XXI. Octobris, A. D. MDCCCLXVI, Habiti, et a Sede Apostolica Recogniti, Acta et Decreta, editio altera, Baltimorae, 1894.

Corpus Iuris Cononici, ed. Lipsiensis secunda, post Aemilii Richteri curas... instruxit Aemilius Friedberg, 2 vols., *Lipsiae,* 1879-1881.

Decretales D. Gregorii Papae IX suae integritati una cum glossis restitutae, cum privilegio Gregorii XIII, Pont. Max., et aliorum Principum, Romae, 1582.

Decretum Gratiani Emendatum et Notationibus Illustratum una cum glossis, Gregorii XIII Pont. Max., iussu editum, 2 vols., Romae, 1582

Enchiridion Symbolorum definitionum et declarationum de rebus fidei et morum, Denzinger-Bannwart-Umberg, editio 21.-23., Friburgi Brisgoviae: Herder Co., 1937.

Jaffé, Philippus, *Regesta Pontificum Romanorum ab Condita Ecclesiae ad annum post Christum natum MCXCVIII,* 2. ed correcta et aucta (ab condita *Ecclesiae ad annum DXC,* ed. Kaltenbrunner; *ab anno DXC ad annum DCCCLXXXII,* ed. Ewald; *ab anno DCCCLXXXII.* ed. Loewenfeld), 2 vols. in 1, Lipsiae, 1885-1888.

Liber Sextus Decretalium D. Bonifacii Papae VIII, una cum Clementinis et Extravagantibus tum D. Joannis XXII tum Communibus, una cum earum glossis, cum privilegio Gregorii XIII, Pont. Max., et aliorum Principum, Romae, 1582.

Mansi, J. D., *Sacrorum Conciliorum Nova et Amplissima Collectio,* 53 vols. in 60 Parisiis, Arnhem, Lipsiae, 1901-1927.

Monumenta Germaniae Historica, Legum Sectio III, Concilia aevi Merovingici, ed. Fridericus Maassen, Hannoveriae, 1893.

Potthast, Augustus, *Regesta Pontificum Romanorum inde ab anno post Christum natum MCXCVIII ad annum MCCCIV,* 2 vols., Berolini, 1874-1875.

Thesaurus Resolutionum Sacrae Congregationis Concilii, 167 vols, Romae, 1718-1908

AUTHORS

Abbas Panormitanus (Nicolaus de Tudeschis), *Omnia Quae Extant Com mentaria in Decretales,* 5 vols. in 7, Venetiis, 1588.

Ayrinhac, H. A.,*Constitution of the Church in the new Code of Canon Law,* New York: Benziger, 1925.

[Bachofen], Charles Augustine, *A Commentary on the New Code of Canon Law,* 8 vols., 1, 6. ed., 1931; Vol. II, 6. ed., 1936, St Louis: Herder & Co.

Badii, Caesar, *Institutiones Iuris Canonici in usum Scholarum,* 3. ed., 2 vols., Florentiae: Libreria Editrice Fiorentina, 1921-1922.

Barraclough, Geoffrey, *Papal Provisions,* Oxford: Basil Blackwell, 1935.

Bastnagel, Clement V., *The Appointment of Parochial Adjutants and Assistants,* The Catholic University of America Canon Law Studies, n. 58, Washington, D. C.,: The Catholic University of America, 1930.

Benedictus, XIV, *De Synodo Dioecesana,* 2. ed., 2 vols., Mechliniae, 1842.

Beste, Udalricus, *Introductio in Codicem,* Collegeville, Minn.: St. John's Abbey Press, 1938.

Blat, Albertus, *Commentarium Textus Codicis Iuris Canonici,* 5 vols. in 7, Vol. II, 2. ed., 1921, Romae: Collegio "Angelico."

Bouix, Dominicus, *Tractatus de Principiis Iuris Canonici,* Parisiis, 1852.

———, *Tractatus de Episcopo,* 2. ed., 2 vols., Parisiis, 1873

Campagna, Angelo, *Il Vicario Generale de L. Vescovo,* The Catholic University of America Canon Law Studies, n. 66, Washington, D.C.: The Catholic University of America, 1931.

Cappello, Felix, *Summa Iuris Canonici,* 3 vols., Vol. I, 3. ed., 1938, Vol. II, 3. ed., 1939; Vol. III, 1936, Romae: Apud Aedes Universitatis Gregorianae.

Castillo, Cayo, *Disertacion Historico-Canonica sobre la Potestad del Cabildo en Sede Vacante o Impedida del Vicario Capitular,* The Catholic University of America Canon Law Studies, n. 4, Washington, D. C.: The Catholic University of America, .1919 (1918).

Cavagnis, Felix, *Institutiones Iuris Publici Ecclesiastici,* 2 vols. in 1, Romae, 1882.

Chelodi, Ioannes, *Ius de Personis iuxta Codicem Iuris Canonici,* 2. ed., Tridenti: Libr. Tridentum, 1927.

Cicognani, Amleto, *Canon Law,* authorized English version, by J. O'Hara and F. Brennan, Philadelphia: Dolphin Press, 1934.

Claeys Bouuaert, *De Canonica Cleri Saecularis Obedientia,* Lovanii, 1904.

Claeys Bouuaert, F.—Simenon, G., *Manuale Iuris Canonici ad usum Seminariorum,* 3 vols., Vol. I, 3. ed., 1930, Gandae et Leodii: Dessain.

Coady, John, *The Appointment of Pastors,* The Catholic University of America Canon Law Studies, n. 52, Washington, D.C.: The Catholic University of America, 1929.

Cocchi, Guidus, *Commentarium in Codicem Iuris Canonici ad Usum Scholarum,* 5 vols. in 8, Vol. II, 3. ed., 1930, Taurinorum Augustae: Marietti.

Coronata, Matthaeus Conte a, *Institutiones Iuris Canonici ad usum Utriusque Cleri et Scholarum,* 5 Vols., Vol I, 2. ed., 1939; Vol. III, 1933, Taurini: Marietti.

D'Angelo, Sosio, *La Curia Dioecesana a norma del Codice di Diritto Canonico,* Giarre (Sicilia): Lisi, 1922.

De Angelis, Philippus, *Praelectiones Iuris Canonici,* 6 vols., Romae: Ex Typographia della Pace, 1877-1878.

De Camillis, Joseph, *Institutiones Juris Canonici,* 3 Vols., vol. I, 1868, Parisiis: Vives.

De Meester, Alphonsis, *Juris Canonici et Juris Canonico-Civilis Compendium,* 3 vols. in 4. ed, nova, Brugis: Sumptibus et Typis Societatis Sancti Augustini, 1921-1928.

Donnellan, Thomas A., *The Obligation of the Missa pro Populo,* The Caoholic University of America Canon Law Studies, n. 155, Washington, D.C.: The Catholic University of America Press, 1942.

Dubé, Arthur J., *The General Principles for the Reckoning of Time in Canon Law,* The Catholic University of America Canon Law Studies, n. 144, Washington, D.C.: The Catholic University of America Press, 1941.

Fagnanus, Prosper, *Commentaria in Quinque Libros Decretalium,* 5 vols. in 3, Coloniae Allobrogum, 1759.

Ferraris, Lucius, *Prompta Bibliotheca Canonica, Iuridica, Moralis, Theologica, necnon Ascetica, Polemica, Rubricistica, Historica,* 9 vols., Romae, 1885-1899.

Garcia Nicolaus, *Tractotus de Beneficiis,* Coloniae Allobrogum, 1936.

Gasparri, P., *Tractatus Canonicus de Sacra Ordinatione,* 2 vols., Parisiis, 1893-1894.

Gluck, I., *Commentario alle Pandette,* 2 vols. Milano, 1888.

Haydt, John J., *Reserved Benefices,* The Catholic University of America Canon Law Studies, n. 161, Washington, D.C.: The Catholic University of America Press, 1942.

Hermes, Henricus, *Dissertatio Historico-Cononica de Capitulo Sede Vacante vel Impedita et de Vicario Capitulari,* Lovanii: Valinthout Fratres, 1873.

Hinschius, Paul, *System des katholischen Kirchenrechts,* 4 vols., Berlin, 1869-1888.

Hostiensis, Cardinalis (Henricus de Segusio), *Commentaria in Quinque Decretalium Libros,* 5 vols. in 3, Venetiis, 1581.

Jaeger, Leo Arnold, *The Administration of Vacant and Quasi-Vacant Dioceses in the United States,* The Catholic University of America Canon Law Studies, n. 81, Washington, D.C.: The Catholic University of America, 1936.

Klekotka, Peter J., *Diocesan Consultors,* The Catholic University of America Canon Law Studies, n. 8, Washington, D.C.: The Catholic University of America, 1920.

LeBuffe, Francis P.—Hayes, James V., *Jurisprudence,* 3 ed., New York; Fordham University Press, 1938.

Lega, M.—Bartoccetti, V., *Commentarius in Iudicia Ecclesiastica,* 3 vols., Romae: Anonima Libreria Catolica-Italiana, 1938-1941.

McBride, James T., ***Incardination and Excardination of Seculars,*** The Catholic University of America Canon Law Studies, n. 145, Washington, D.C.: The Catholic University of America Press, 1941.

McDonough, Thomas J., ***Apostolic Administrators,*** The Catholic University of America Canon Law Studies, n. 139, Washington, D.C.: The Catholic University of America Press, 1941.

Maroto, Philippus, ***Institutiones Iuris Canonici ad Norman Novi Codicis,*** 2 vols., Madrid: Editorial del Corazon de Maria, 1918.

Migne, J. P., ***Patrologiae Cursus Completus, Series Graeca,*** 161 vols., Parisiis, 1856-1864.

———, ***Patrologiae Cursus Completus, Series Latina,*** 221 vols., Parisiis, 1844-1864.

Moersdorf, Klaus, ***Die Rechtssprache des Codex Iuris Canonici,*** Veroeffentlichungen der Goerresgesellschaft, Sektion fuer Rechts-und Staats-wissenschaft, Heft. 74, Paderborn: Schoeningh, 1937.

Neuberger, Nicholas J., ***Canon*** 6, The Catholic University of America Canon Law Studies, n. 44, Washington, D.C.: The Catholic University of America, 1927.

Ojetti, Benedictus, ***Commentarium in Codicem Iuris Canonici,*** 4 vols., Romae: Universitas Gregoriana, 1927-1931.

Oesterle, Gerardus, ***Praelectiones Iuris Canonici,*** Vol. I, 1931, Romae: Collegio S. Anselmi.

Ottaviani, Alaphridus, ***Institutiones Iuris Publici Ecclesiastici,*** 2. ed., 2 vols., Typis Polyglottis Vaticanis, 1935-1936.

Parsons, Anscar, ***Canonical Elections,*** The Catholic University of America Canon Law Studies, n. 118, Washington, D.C.: The Catholic University of America Press, 1939.

Perugini, Angelus, ***Concordata Vigentia, notis historicis et iuridicis declarata,*** Romae: apud Custodiam Librariam Pont. Instituti Utriusque Iuris, 1934.

Pirhing Ernricus, ***Ius Canonicum in Quinque Libros Decretalium Distributum,*** Dillingae, 1674-1678.

Pistocchi, Marius, ***De Re Beneficiali,*** Taurini: Marietti, 1928.

Poulet, Dom. Charles, ***A History of the Catholic Church,*** authorized translation and adaption from the fourth French edition by the Rev. Sidney A. Raemers, 2 vols., St. Louis: Herder & Co., 1943.

Prince, John E., ***The Diocesan Chancellor,*** The Catholic University of America Canon Law Studies, n. 167, Washington, D.C.: The Catholic University of America Press, 1942.

Prummer, Dominicus, ***Manuale Iuris Canonici in Usum Scholarum,*** 3. ed., Friburgi Brisgoviae, 1922.

Raus, J. B., ***Institutiones Canonicae iuxta Novum Codicem Juris,*** ed. altera, Lugduni-Parisiis: Typis Emmanuelis Vitte, 1931.

Reiffenstuel, Anacletus, ***Jus Canonicum Universum,*** 5 vols. in 7, Venetiis, 1735.

Riganti, Ioannes B., ***Commentaria in regulas, constitutiones, et ordinationes cancellariae apostolicae,*** opus posthumum, 4 vols. in 2, Coloniae Allobrogum, 1751.

Roberti, Franciscus, *De Processibus,* 2 vols., Romac: Apud Acdcs Facultatis Iuridicae ad S. Apollinaris, 1926.

Rufinus, *Die Summa des Magister Rufinus,* ed. Heinrich Singer, Paderborn, 1902.

Ryan, Gerald A., *Principles of Episcopal Jurisdiction,* The Catholic University of America Canon Law Studies, n. 120, Washington, D.C.: The Catholic University of America Press, 1939.

Sanguinetti, Sebastiano, *Iuris Ecclesiastici Privati Institutiones,* Romae, 1884.

Santi, Franciscus, *Praelectiones Iuris Canonici,* 5 vols. in 2, Ratisbonae: Pustet, 1886.

Schmalzgrueber, Franciscus, *Ius Ecclesiasticum Universum,* 5 vols. in 12, Romae, 1843-1845.

Sipos, Stephonus, *Enchiridion Iuris Canonici,* 3. ed., Pecs: "Haladaas R.T.," 1936.

Smith, S. B., *Elements of Ecclesiastical Law,* 3 vols., Vol. I, 9. ed., 1887; Vol. II, 5. ed., 1887; Vol. III, 3. ed., 1888; New York: Benziger.

———, *Notes on the Second Plenary Council of Baltimore,* New York, 1874.

Solieri, Franciscus, *Institutiones Iuris Ecclesiastici,* 2. ed., Romae: Pustet, 1921.

Thomas Aquinas, St., *Opera Omnia,* 32 vols., Parisiis: Vives, 1871-1879:
Commentarium in IV Libros Sententiarum;
Summa Theologica.

Thomassinus, Ludovicus, *Vetus et Nova Ecclesiae Disciplina circa Beneficia et Beneficiarios,* 10 vols., Moguntiae, 1787.

Tobin, Thomas I., *De Officiali Curiae Dioecesanae,* Romae: Apud Aedes Pontificiae Universitatis Gregorianae, 1936.

Toso, Albertus, *Ad Codicem Iuris Canonici Commentaria Minora,* 5 vols., Vol. I, 1921, Tiferni Tiberini: Typographica Vinciana.

Van-Espen, Zegerus Bernardus, *Ius Ecclesiasticum Universum,* 5 vols., Lovanii, 1753.

Van Hove, A., *De Consuetudine—De Temporis Supputatione,* Mechliniae: Dessain, 1933.

Vermeersch, Arthurus—Creusen, Josephus, *Epitome Iuris Canonici,* 3 vols., Vol. I, 6. ed., 1937; Vol. II, 5. ed., 1934; Vol. III, 5. ed., 1936, Romae, Mechliniae: H. Dessain.

Wernz, Franciscus, *Ius Decretalium ad usum Praelectionum in Scholis Textus Iuris Canonici, sive Iuris Decretalium,* 3. ed., 6 vols., Prati, 1915.

Wernz, Franciscus—Vidal, Petrus, *Ius Canonicum ad Norman Codicis Exactum,* 7 vols. in 8, Vol. II, 2. ed., 1928; Vol. VI, 1927, Romae: Apud Aedes Universitatis Gregorianae.

Zaplotnik, Ioannes Leo, *De Vicariis Foraneis,* The Catholic University of America Canon Law Studies, n. 47, Washington, D.C.: The Catholic University of America, 1927.

Articles

Hilling, N., "Kirchliches *officum* und *potestas ordnaria,*" — *Archiv fuer katholiches Kirchenrecht,* CXVII (1937), 433-435.

Larraona, A., "De Electoribus Religiosorum,"—*Commentarium pro Religiosis,* VIII (1927), 284-295.

Lo Gasso, I., "De incompatibilitate officiorum,"—*Periodica,* XXIV (1935), 34-36.

Simenon, G., "Renuntiatio Officiorum Ecclesiasticorum,"—*Revue Ecclésiastique de Liége,* XXII (1930-1931), 182-186.

Sipos, S., "Ad officium sacrum an requiritur potestas ordinaria,"—*Jus Pontificium,* XVI, (1936) 67-69.

Van de Kerekhove, M., " De Notione Iurisdictionis in Iure Romano,"—*Jus Pontificium,* XVI (1936), 49-65.

Vermeersch, A., "De tempore utili electionis faciendae,"—*Periodica,* XIII (1924), 71-72.

———, "De vera Familiaritas Ratione et de Familiaribus,"—*Periodica,* III (1914), 269-276.

———, "Familiares in genere et in Codice,"—*Periodica,* XIX (1930), 63-67.

Periodicals

Archiv fuer katholisches Kirchenrecht, Innsbruck, 1857-1861; Mainz, 1862—

Commentarium pro Religiosis, Romae, 1920—; from 1935; *Commentarium pro Religiosis et Missionariis.*

Jurist, The, Washington, D.C., 1941—

Jus Pontificium, Romae, 1921—

Periodica de Religiosis et Missionariis, Brugis, 1905-1919; ab anno 1920, *Periodica de Re Canonica et Morali utilia praesertim Religiosis et Missionariis,* Brugis, 1920-1927; ab anno 1927, *Periodica de Re Morali, Canonica, Liturgica,* Brugis, 1927-1936, et Romae, 1937—

Revue Ecclesiastique de Liege, Leodii, 1908—

ABBREVIATIONS

AAS—Acta Apostolicae Sedis.
c.—canon seu caput (iuris antiqui).
can.—canon (novi Codciis).
Fontes—Codicis Iuris Canonici Fontes.
Codex I. C.—Codex Iuris Cnaonici.
JE—Jaffe, *Regesta Pontificum Romanorum* (edited by Ewald: from 590 to 882).
JK—Jaffé, *op. cit.* (edited by Kaltenbrunner: from 33 to 590).
JL—Jaffe, *op. cit.* (edited by Loewenfeld: from 882 to 1198).
Mansi—*Sacrorum Conciliorum Nova et Amplissima Collectio.*
Periodica—Periodica de Re Canonica, Morali, Liturgica.
Potthast—*Regesta Pontificum Romanorum.*
S. C. Conc.—Sacra Congregatio Concilii.
S. C. Consist.—Sacra Congregatio Consistorialis.
Thesaurus—Theasurus Resolutionum Sacre Congregationis Concilii.

ALPHABETICAL INDEX

BIOGRAPHICAL NOTE

Joseph Leroy Manning was born on February 27, 1915, in Houston, Texas. He attended the Public Schools of Terryville and Choat, and St. Leo's and St. Henry's Parochial Schools in San Antonio, Texas. He entered St. John's Archdiocesan Seminary in that city in the fall of 1929, where he completed his preparatory and theological studies, and was ordained to the priesthood on April 2, 1940. At the request of his Most Reverend Archbishop he entered the Graduate School of Canon Law at the Catholic University of America in the fall of 1942. From this School he received the degree of Baccalaureate in Canon Law in May of 1943 and the degree of Licentiate in Canon Law in May of 1944.

CANON LAW STUDIES*

1. FRERIKS, REV. CELESTINE A., C.PP.S., J.C.D., Religious Congregations in Their External Relations, 121 pp., '916.
2. GALLIHER, REV. DANIEL M., O.P., J.C.D., Canonical Elections, 117 pp., 1917.
3. BORKOWSKI, REV. AURELIUS L., O.F.M., J.C.D., De Confraternitatibus Ecclesiasticis, 136 pp., 1918.
4. CASTILLO, REV. CAYO, J.C.D., Disertacion Historico-Canonica sobre la Potestod del Cabildo en Sede Vacante o Impedida del Vicario Capitular, 99 pp., 1919 (1918).
5. KUBELBECK, REV. WILLIAM J., S.T.B., J.C.D., The Sacred Penitentiaria and Its Relation to Faculties of Ordinaries and Priests, 129 pp., 1918.
6. PETROVITS, REV. JOSEPH J. C., S.T.D., J.C.D., The New Church Law on Matrimony, X-461, pp., 1919.
7. HICKEY, REV. JOHN J., S.T.B., J.C.D., Irregularities and Simple Impediments in the New Code of Canon Law, 100 pp., 1920.
8. KLEKOTKA, REV. PETER J., S.T.B., J.C.D., Diocesan Consultors, 179 pp., 1920.
9. WANENMACHER, REV. FRANCIS, J.C.D., The Evidence in Ecclesiastical Procedure Affecting the Marriage Bond, 1920 (Printed 1935).
10. GOLDEN, REV. HENRY FRANCIS, J.C.D., Parochial Benefices in the New Code, IV-119 pp., 1921 (Printed 1925).
11. KOUDELKA, REV. CHARLES J., J.C.D., Pastors, Their Rights and Duties According to the New Code of Canon Law, 211 pp., 1921.
12. MELO, REV. ANTONIUS, O.F.M., J.C.D., De Exemptione Regularium, X-188 pp., 1921.
13. SCHAAF, REV. VALENTINE THEODORE, O.F.M., S.T.B., J.C.D., The Cloister, X-180 pp., 1921.
14. BURKE, REV. THOMAS JOSEPH, S.T.D, J.C.D., Competence in Ecclesiastical Tribunals, IV-117 pp., 1922.
15. LEECH, REV. GEORGE LEO, J.C.D., A Comparative Study of the Constitution "Apostolicae Sedis" and the "Codex Juris Canonici," 179 pp., 1922.
16. MOTRY, REV. HUBERT LOUIS, S.T.D., J.C.D., Diocesan Faculties According to the Code of Canon Law, II-167 pp., 1922.
17. MURPHY, REV. GEORGE LAWRENCE, J.C.D., Delinquencies and Penalties in the Administration and the Reception of the Sacraments, IV-121 pp., 1923.
18. O'REILLY, REV. JOHN ANTHONY, S.T.B., J.C.D., Ecclesiastical Sepulture in the New Code of Canon Law, 11-129 pp., 1923.
19. MICHALICKA, REV. WENCESLAS CYRIL, O.S.B. J.C.D. Judicial Procedure in Dismissal of Clerical Exempt Religious, 107 pp., 1923.
20. DARGIN, REV. EDWARD VINCENT, S.T.B, J.C.D., Reserved Cases According to the Code of Canon Law, IV-103 pp., 1924.

* Below n. 100 only the following numbers are still available: Nos. 25, 57 and 75. Beginning with n. 100 only the following are unavailable: Nos. 100-111 inclusive, 113 and 115-117 inclusive.

21. GODFREY, REV. JOHN A., S.T.B., J.C.D., The Right of Patronage According to the Code of Canon Law, 153 pp., 1924.

22. HAGEDORN, REV. FRANCIS EDWARD, J.C.D., General Legislation on Indulgences, II-154 pp., 1924.

23. KING, REV. JAMES IGNATIUS, J.C.D., The Administration of the Sacraments to Dying, Non-Catholics, V-141 pp., 1924.

24. WINSLOW, REV. FRANCIS JOSEPH, O.F.M., J.C.D., Vicars and Prefects Apostolic, IV-149 pp., 1924.

25. CORREA, REV. JOSE SERVELION, S.T.L., J.C.D., La Potestad Legislativa de la Iglesia Catolica, IV-127 pp., 1925.

26. DUGAN, REV. HENRY FRANCIS, A.M., J.C.D., The Judiciary Department of the Diocesan Curia, 87 pp., 1925.

27. KELLER, REV. CHARLES FREDERICK, S.T.B., J.C.D., Mass Stipends, 167 pp., 1925.

28. PASCHANG, REV. JOHN LINUS, J.C.D. The Sacramentals According to the Code of Canon Law, 129 pp., 1925.

29. PIONTEK, REV. CYRILLUS, O.F.M., S.T.B., J.C.D., De Indulto Exclaustrationis necnon Saecularizationis, XIII-289 pp., 1925.

30. KEARNEY, REV. RICHARD JOSEPH, S.T.B., J.C.D., Sponsors at Baptism According to the Code of Canon Law, IV-127 pp., 1925.

31. BARTLETT, REV. CHESTER JOSEPH, A.M., LL.B., J.C.D., The Tenure of Parochial Property in the United States of America, V-108 pp., 1926.

32. KILKER, REV. ADRIAN JEROME, J.C.D., Extreme Unction, V-425 pp., 1926.

33. MCCORMICK, REV. ROBERT EMMETT, J.C.D., Confessors of Religious, VIII-266 pp., 1926.

34. MILLER, REV. NEWTON THOMAS, J.C.D., Founded Masses According to the Code of Canon Law, VII-93 pp., 1926.

35. ROELKER, REV. EDWARD G., S.T.D., J.C.D., Principles of Privilege According to the Code of Canon Law, XI-166 pp., 1926.

36. BAKALARCZYK, REV. RICHARDUS, M.I.C., J.U.D., De Novitiatu, VIII-208 pp., 1927.

37. PIZZUTI, REV. LAWRENCE, O.F.M., J.U.L., De Parochis Religiosis, 1927. (Not Printed.)

38. BLILEY, REV. NICHOLAS MARTIN, O.S.B., J.C.D., Altars According to the Code of Canon Law, XIX-132 pp., 1927.

39. BROWN, MR. BRENDAN FRANCIS, A.B., LL. M., J.U.D., The Canonical Juristic Personality with Special Reference to its Status in the United States of America, V-212 pp., 1927.

40. CAVANAUGH, REV. WILLIAM THOMAS, C.P., J.U.D., The Reservation of the Blessed Sacrament, VIII-101 pp., 1927.

41. DOHENY, REV. WILLIAM J. C.S.C., A.B., J.U.D. Church Property: Modes of Acquistion, X-118 pp., 1927.

42. FELDHAUS, REV. ALOYSIUS *H.*, C.P.P.S., J.C.D., Oratories, IX-141 pp., 1927.

43. KELLY, REV. JAMES PATRICK, A.B., J.C.D., The Jurisdiction of the Simple Confessor, X-208 pp., 1927.

44. Neuberger, Rev. Nicholas J., J.C.D., Canon 6 or the Relation of the Codex Juris Canonici to the Preceding Legislation, V-95 pp., 1927.

45. O'Keefe, Rev. Gerald Mitchell, J.C.D., Matrimonial Dispensations, Powers of Bishops, Priests, and Confessors, VIII-232 pp., 1927.

46. Quigley, Rev. Joseph A. M., A.B., J.C.D., Condemned Societies, 139 pp., 1927.

47. Zaplotnik, Rev. Johannes Leo, J.C.D., De Vicariis Foraneis, X-142 pp., 1927.

48. Duskie, Rev. John Aloysius, A.B., J.C.D., The Canonical Status of the Orientals in the United States, VIII-196 pp., 1928.

49. Hyland, Rev. Francis Edward, J.C.D., Excommunication, Its Nature, Historical Development and Effects, VIII-181 pp., 1928.

50. Reinmann, Rev. Gerald Joseph, O.M.C., J.C.D., The Third Order Secular of Saint Francis, 201 pp., 1928.

51. Schenk, Rev. Francis J., J.C.D., The Matrimonial Impediments of Mixed Religion and Disparity of Cult, XVI-318 pp., 1929.

52. Coady, Rev. John Joseph, S.T.D., J.U.D., A.M., The Appointment of Pastors, VIII-150 pp., 1929.

53. Kay, Rev. Thomas Henry, J.C.D., Competence in Matrimonial Procedure, VIII-164 pp., 1929.

54. Turner, Rev. Sidney Joseph, C.P., J.U.D., the Vow of Poverty, XLIX-217 pp., 1929.

55. Kearney, Rev. Raymond A., A.B., S.T.D., J.C.D., The Principles of Delegation, VII-149 pp., 1929.

56. Conran, Rev. Edward James, A.B., J.C.D., The Interdict, V-163 pp., 1930.

57. O'Neill, Rev. William H., J.C.D., Papal Rescripts of Favor, VII-218 pp., 1930.

58. Bastnagel, Rev. Clement Vincent, J.U.D., The Appointment of Parochial Adjutants and Assistants, XV-257 pp., 1930.

59. Ferré,Rev. William A., A.B., J.C.D., Stole Fees, V-136 pp., 1930.

60. Costello, Rev. John Michael, A.B., J.C.D., Domicile and Quasi-Domicile, VII-201 pp., 1930.

61. Kremer, Rev. Michael Nicholas, A.B, S.T.B., J.C.D., Church Support in the United States, VI-136 pp., 1930.

62. Angulo, Rev. Luis, C.M., J.C.D., Legislation de la Iglesia sobre la intencion en la application de la Santa Misa, VII-104 pp., 1931.

63. Frey, Rev. Wolfgang Norbert, O.S.B., J.C.D., The Act of Religious Profession, VIII-174 pp., 1931.

64. Roberts, Rev. James Brendan, A.B, J.C.D., The Banns of Marriage, XIV-140 pp., 1931.

65. Ryder, Rev. Raymond Aloysius, A.B., J.C.D., Simony, IX-151 pp., 1931.

66. Campagna, Rev. Angelo, Pœ.D., J.U.D., I Vicario General del Vescovo. VII-205 pp., 1931.

67. Cox, Rev. Joseph Godfrey, A.B., J.C.D., The Administration of Seminaries, VI-124 pp., 1931.

68. GREGORY, REV. DONALD J., J.U.D., The Pauline Privilege, XV-165 pp., 1931.
69. DONOHUE, REV. JOHN F., J.C.D., The Impediment of Crime, VII-110 pp., 1931.
70. DOOLEY, REV. EUGENE A., O.M.I., J.C.D., Church Law on Sacred Relics, IX-143 pp., 1931.
71. ORTH, REV. CLEMENT RAYMOND, O.M.C., J.C.D., The Approbation of Religious Institutes, 171 pp., 1931.
72. PERNICONE, REV. JOSEPH M., A.B., J.C.D., The Ecclesiastical Prohibition of Books, XII-267 pp., 1932.
73. CLINTON, REV. CONNELL, A.B., J.C.D., The Paschal Precept, IX-108 pp., 1932.
74. DONNELLY, REV. FRANCIS B., A.M., S.T.L., J.C.D., The Diocesan Synod, VIIII-125 pp., 1932.
75. TORRENTE, REV. CAMILO, C.M.F., J.C.D., Las Procesiones Sagradas, V-145 pp., 1932.
76. MURPHY, REV. EDWIN J., C.PP.S., J.C.D., Suspension Ex Informata Conscientia, XI-122 pp., 1932.
77. MACKENZIE, REV. ERIC F., A.M., S.T.L., J.C.D., The Delict of Heresy in its Commission, Penalization, Absolution, VII-124 pp., 1932.
78. LYONS, REV. AVITUS E., S.T.B., J.C.D., The Collegiate Tribunal of First Instance, XI-147 pp., 1932.
79. CONNOLLY, REV. THOMAS A., J.C.D., Appeals, XI-195 pp., 1932.
80. SANGMEISTER, REV. JOSEPH V., A.B., J.C.D., Force and Fear as Precluding Matrimonial Consent V-211 pp., 3192.
81. JAEGER, REV. LEO A., A.B., J.C.D., The Administration of Vacant and Quasi-Vacant Episcopal Sees in the United States, IX-229 pp., 1932.
82. RIMLINGER, REV. HERBERT T., J.C.D., Error Invalidating Matrimonial Consent, VII-79 pp., 1932.
83. BARRETT, REV. JOHN D. M., S.S., J.C.D., A Comparative Study of the Third Plenary Council of Baltimore and the Code, IX-221 pp., 1932.
84. CARBERRY, REV. JOHN J., Ph.D., S.T.D. J.C.D., The Juridical Form of Marriage, X-177 pp, 1934
85. DOLAN, REV. JOHN L., A.B., J.C.D., The Defensor Vinculi, XI-157 pp., 1934.
86. HANNAN, REV. JEROME D., A.M., S.T.D., LL.B., J.C.D., the Canon Law of Wills, IX-517 pp., 1934.
87. LEMIEUX, REV. DELISE A., A.M., J.C.D., The Sentence in Ecclesiastical Procedure, IX-131 pp., 1934.
88. O'ROURKE, REV. JAMES J., A.B., J.C.D., Parish Registers, VII-109 pp., 1934.
89. TIMLIN, REV. BARTHOLOMEW, O.F.M., A.M., J.C.D., Conditional Matrimonial Consent, X-381 pp., 1934.
90. WAHL, REV. FRANCIS X., A.B., J.C.D., The Matrimonial Impediments of Consanguinity and Affinity, VI-125 pp., 1934.
91. WHITE, REV. ROBERT J., A.B., LL.B., S.T.B., J.C.D., Canonical Ante-Nupital Promises and the Civil Law, VI-152 pp., 1934.

92. HERRERA, REV. ANTONIO PARRA, O.C.D., J.C.D., Legislacion Ecclesiastica sobra el Ayuno y la Abstinencia, XI-191 pp. 1935.
93. KENNEDY, REV. EDWIN J., J.C.D., The Special Matrimonial Process in Cases of Evident Nullity, X-165 pp., 1935.
94. MANNING, REV. JOHN J., A.B., J.C.D., Presumption of Law in Motrimonial Procedure, XI-111 pp., 1935.
95. MOEDER, REV. JOHN M., J.C.D., The Proper Bishop for Ordination and Dimissorial Letters, VII-135 pp., 1935.
96. O'MARA, REV. WILLIAM A., A.B., J.C.D., Canonical Causes for Matrimonial Dispensations, IX-155 pp., 1935.
97. REILLY, REV. PETER, J.C.D., Residence of Pastors, IX-81 pp., 1935.
98. SMITH, REV. MARINER T., O.P., S.T.Lr., J.C.D., The Penal Law for Religious, VII-169 pp., 1935.
99. WHALEN, REV. DONALD W., A.M., J.C.D., The Value of Testimonial Evidence in Matrimonial Procedure, XIII-297 pp., 1935.
100. CLEARY, REV. JOSEPH F., J.C.D., Canonical Limitations on the Alienation of Church Property, VIII-141 pp., 1936.
101. GLYNN, REV. JOHN C., J.C.D., The Promoter of Justice, XX-337 pp., 1936.
102. BRENNAN, REV. JAMES H., S.S., M.A., S.T.B., J.C.D., The Simple Convalidation of Marriage, VI-135 pp., 1937.
103. BRUNINI, REV. JOSEPH BERNARD, J.C.D., The Clerical Obligations of Canons 139 and 142, X-121, pp., 1937.
104. CONNOR, REV. MAURICE, A.B., J.C.D., The Administrative Removal of Pastors, VIII-159 pp., 1937.
105. GUILFOYLE, REV. MERLIN JOSEPH, J.C.D., Custom, XI-144 pp., 1937.
106. HUGHES, REV. JAMES AUSTIN, A.B., A.M., J.C.D., Witnesses in Criminal Trials of Clerics, IX-140 pp., 1937.
107. JANSEN, REV. RAYMOND J., A.B., S.T.L., J.C.D., Canonical Provisions for Catechetical Instruction, VII-153 pp., 1937.
108. KEALY, REV. JOHN JAMES, A.B., J.C.D., The Introductory Libellus in Church Court Procedure, XI-121 pp., 1937.
109. MCMANUS, REV., JAMES EDWARD, C.SS.R., J.C.D., The Administration of Temporal Goods in Religious Institutes, XVI-196 pp., 1937.
110. MORIAROTY, REV. EUGENE JAMES, J.C.D., Oathes in Ecclesiastical Courts, X-115 pp., 1937.
111. RAINER, REV. ELIGIUS GEORGE, C.SS.R., J.C.D., Suspension of Clerics, XVII-249 pp., 1937.
112. REILLY, REV. THOMAS F., C.SS.R., J.C.D., Visitation of Religious, VI-195 pp., 1938.
113. MORIARITY, REV. FRANCIS E., C.SS.R., J.C.D., The Extraordinary Absolution from Censures, XV-334 pp., 1938.
114. CONNOLLY, REV. NICHOLAS P., J.C.D., The Canonical Erection of Parishes, X-132 pp., 1938.
115. DONOVAN, REV. JAMES JOSEPH, J.C.D., The Pastor's Obligation in Prenuptial Investigation, XII-322 pp., 1938.

116. Harrigan, Rev. Robert J., M.A., S.T.B., J.C.D., The Radical Sanation of Invalid Marriages, VIII-208 pp., 1938.
117. Boffa, Rev. Conrad Humbert, J.C.D., Canonical Provisions for Catholic Schools, VII-211 pp., 1939.
118. Parsons, Rev. Anscar John, O.M.Cap., J.C.D., Canonical Elections, XII-236 pp., 1939.
119. Reilly, Rev. Edward Michael, A.B., J.C.D., The General Norms of Dispensation, XII-156 pp., 1939.
120. Ryan, Rev. Gerald Aloysius, A.B., J.C.D., Principles of Episcopal Jurisdiction, XII-172 pp., 1939.
121. Burton, Rev. Francis James, C.S.C., A.B., J.C.D., A Commentary on Canon 1125, X-222 pp., 1940.
122. Miaskiewicz, Rev. Francis Sigimund, J.C.D., Supplied Jurisdiction According to Canon 209, XII-340 pp., 1940.
123. Rice, Rev. Patrick William, A.B., J.C.D., Proof of Death in Prenuptial Investigation, VIII-156 pp., 1940.
124. Anglin, Rev. Thomas Francis, M.S. J.C.D., The Eucharistic Fast, VIII-183 pp., 1941.
125. Coleman, Rev. John Jerome, J.C.D., The Minister of Confirmation, VI-153 pp., 1941.
126. Downs, Rev. Joseph Emmanuel, A.B., J.C.D., The Concept of Clerical Immunity, XI-163 pp., 1941.
127. Esswein, Rev. Anthony Albert, J.C.D., Extrajudicial Penal Powers of Ecclesiastical Superiors, X-144 pp., 1941.
128. Farrell, Rev. Benjamin Francis, M.A., S.T.L., J.C.D., The Rights and Duties of the Local Ordinary Regarding Congregations of Women Religious of Pontifical Approval, pp., 1941.
129. Feeney, Rev. Thomas John, A.B., S.T.L., J.C.D., Restitutio in Integrum, VI-169 pp., 1941.
130. Findlay, Rev. Stephen William, O.S.B., A.B., J.C.D., Canonical Norms Governing the Deposition and Degradation of Clerics, XVII-279 pp. 1941.
131. Goodwine, Rev. John, A.B, S.T.L., J.C.D., The Right of the Church to Acquire Property, VIII-119 pp., 1941.
132. Heston, Rev. Edward Louis, C.S.C., Ph.D., S.T.D., J.CD., The Alienation of Church Property in the United States, XII-222 pp., 1941.
133. Hogan, Rev. James John, A.B., S.T.L., J.C.D., Judicial Advocates and Procurators, XIII-200 pp., 1941.
134. Kealy, Rev. Thomas M., A.B., Litt.D., J.C.D., Dowry of Women Religious, IX-152 pp., 1941.
135. Keene, Rev. Michael James, O.S.B., J.C.D., Religious Ordinaries and Canon 198, V-164 pp., 1942.
136. Kerin, Rev. Charles A., S.S., M.A., S.T.B., J.C.D., The Privation of Christian Burial, XVI-279 pp., 1941.
137. Louis, Rev. Wi liam Francis, M.A., J.C.D., Diocesan Archives, X-101 pp., 1941.

138. McDevitt, Rev. Gilbert Joseph, A.B., J.C.D., Legitimacy and Legitimation, X-247 pp., 1941.

139. McDonough, Rev. Thomas Joseph, A.B., J.C.D., Apostolic Administrators, X-217 pp., 1941.

140. Meier, Rev. Carl Anthony, A.B., J.C.D., Penal Administration Procedure Against Negligent Pastors, XI-240 pp., 1941.

141. Schmidt, Rev. John Rogg, A.B., J.C.D., The Principles of Authentic Interpretation in Canon 17 of the Code of Canon Law, XII-331 pp., 1941.

142. Slafkosky, Rev. Andrew Leonard, A.B., J.C.D., The Canonical Episcopal Visitation of the Diocese, X-197 pp., 1941.

143. Swoboda Rev. Innocent Robert, O.F.M., J.C.D., Ignorance in Relation to the Imputability of Delicts, IX-271 pp., 1941.

144. Dube, Rev. Arthur Joseph, A.B. J.C.D. The General Principles for the Reckoning of Time in Canon Law, VIII-299 pp., 1941.

145. McBride, Rev. James T., A.B., J.C.D., Incardination and Excardination of Seculars, XX-585 pp., 1941.

146. Krol, Rev. John T., J.C.D., The Defendant in Ecclesiastical Trials, XII-207 pp., 1942.

147. Comyns, Rev. Joseph J., C.SS.R., A.B., J.C.D., Papal and Episcopal Administration of Church Property, XIV-155 pp., 1942.

148. Barry, Rev. Garrett Francis, O.M.I., J.C.D., Violation of the Cloister, XII-260 pp., 1942.

149. Bolduc, Rev. Gatien, C.S.V., A.B., S.T.L. J.C.D., Les Etudes Dans les Religious Clericales, VIII-155 pp., 1942.

150. Boyle, Rev. David John, M.A., J.C.D., The Juridic Effects of Moral Certitude on Pre-Nuptial Guarantees, XII-188 pp., 1942.

151. Canavan, Rev. Walter Joseph, M.A., Litt.D., J.C.D., The Profession of Faith, XII-143 pp., 1942.

152. Desrochers, Rev. Bruno, A.B., Ph.L., S.T.B., J.C.D., Le Prèmier Concile Plenier de Quebec et le Code de Droit Canonique, XIV-186 pp., 1942.

153. Dillon, Rev. Robert Edward, A.B., J.C.D., Common Law Marriage, X-148 pp., 1942.

154. Dodwell, Rev. Edward John, Ph.D., S.T.B., J.C.D., The Time and Place for the Celebration of Marriage, X-156 pp., 1942.

155. Donnellan, Rev. Thomas Andrew, A.B., J.C.D., The Obligation of the Misa pro Populo, VII-131 pp., 1942.

156. Elitz, Rev. Louis Anthony, A.B., J.C.D., Cooperation in Crime, XII-208 pp., 1942.

157. Gass, Rev. Sylvester Francis, M.A., J.C.D., Ecclesiastical Pensions, XI-206 pp., 1942.

158. Guiniven, Rev. John Joseph, C.SS.R., J.C.D., The Precept of Hearing Mass, XIV-188 pp., 1942.

159. Gulczynski, Rev. John Theophilus, J.C.D., The Desecration and Violation of Churches, X-126 pp., 1942.

160. Hammill, Rev. John Leo, M.A., J.C.D., The Obligations of the Traveler According to Canon 14, VIII-204 pp., 1942.

161. Haydt, Rev. John Joseph, A.B., J.C.D., Reserved Benefices, XI-148 pp., 1942.

162. Huser, Rev. Roger John, O.F.M., A.B., J.C.D., The Crime of Abortion in Canon Law, XII-187 pp., 1942.

163. Kearney, Rev. Francis Patrick, A.B., S.T.L., J.C.L., The Principles of Canon 1127.

164. Linahen, Rev. Leo James, S.T.L., J.C.D., De Absolutione Complicis In Peccato Turpi, 114 pp., 1942.

165. McCloskey, Rev. Joseph Aloysius, A.B., J.C.D., The Subject of Ecclesiastical Law According to Canon 12, XVII-246 pp., 1942.

166. O'Neill, Rev. Francis Joseph, C.SS.R., J.C.D., The Dismissal of Religious in Temporary Vows, XIII-220 pp., 1942.

167. Prince, Rev. John Edward, A.B., S.T.D., J.C.D., The Diocesan Chancellor, X-136 pp., 1942.

168. Riesner, Rev. Albert Joseph, C.SS.R., J.C.D., Apostates and Fugitives from Religious Institutes, IX-168, pp., 1942.

169. Stenger, Rev. Joseph Bernard, J.C.D., The Mortgaging of Church Property, 186 pp., 1942.

170. Waldron, Rev. Joseph Francis, A.B., J.C.D., The Minister of Baptism, XII-197 pp., 1942.

171. Willett, Rev. Robert Albert, J.C.D., The Probative Value of Documents in Ecclesiastical Trials, X-124 pp., 1942.

172. Woeber, Rev. Edward Martin, M.A., J.C.D., The Interpellations, XII-161 pp., 1942.

173. Benko, Rev. Matthew Aloysius, O.S.B., M.A., J.C.D., The Abbot *Nullius*, XVI-148 pp., 1943.

174. Christ, Rev. Joseph James, M.A., S.T.L., J.C.D., Dispensation from Vindicative Penalties, XIV-285 pp., 1943.

175. Clancy, Rev. Patrick M. J., O.P., A.B., S.T.Lr., J.C.D., The Local Religiious Superior, X-299 pp., 1943.

176. Clarke, Rev. Thomas James, J.C.D., Parish Societies, XII-147 pp., 1943.

177. Connolly, Rev. John Patrick, S.T.L., J.C.D., Synodal Examiners and Parish Priest Consultors, X-223 pp., 1943.

178. Drumm, Rev. William Martin, A.B., J.C.D., Hospital Chaplains, XII-175 pp., 1943.

179. Flaagan, Rev. Bernard Joseph, A.B., S.T.L, J.C.D., The Canonical Erection of Religious Housse, X-147, pp., 1943.

180. Kelleher, Rev. Stephen Joseph, S. T. B., S.T.B., J.C.D., Discussions with non-Catholics: Canonical Legislation, X-93 pp., 1943.

181. Lewis, Rev. Gordian, C.P., J.C.D., Chaptetrs in Religious Institutes, XII-169 pp., 1943.

182. Marx, Rev. Adolph, J.C.D., The Declaration of Nullity of Marriages Contracted Outside the Church, X-151 pp., 1943.

183. MATULENAS, REV. RAYMOND ANTHONY, O.S.B., A.B., J.C.D., Communication, a Source of Privileges, XII-225 pp., 1943.

184. O'LEARY, REV. CHARLES GERARD, C.SS.R., J.C.D., Religious Dismissed After Perpetual Profession, X-213 pp., 1943.

185. POWER, REV. CORNELIUS MICHAEL, J.C.D., The Blessing of Cemeteries, XII-231 pp., 1943.

186. SHUHLER, REV. RALPH VINCENT, O.S.A., J.C.D., Privilege of Regulars to Absolve and Dispense, XII-195 pp., 1943.

187. ZIOLKOWSKI, REV. THADDEUS STANISLAUS, A.B., J.C.D., The Consecration and Blessing of Churches, XII-151 pp., 1943.

188. HENEGHAN, REV. JOHN JOSEPH, S.T.D., J.C.D., The Marriage of Unworthy Catholics: Conons 1065 and 1066, XVI-213 pp., 1944.

189. CARROLL, REV. COLEMAN FRANCIS, M.A., S.T.L., J.C.L., Charitable Institutions.

190. CIESLUK, REV. JOSEPH EDWARD, PH.B., S.T.L., J.C.L., National Parishes in the United States.

191. COBURN, REV. VINCENT PAUL, A.B., J.C.D., Marriages of Conscience, XII-172 pp., 1944.

192. CONNORS, REV. CHARLES PAUL, C.S.Sp., A.B., J.C.D., Extra-Judicial Procurators in the Code of Canon Law, X-94 pp., 1944.

193. COYLE, REV. PAUL RAYMOND, A.B., J.C.D., Judicial Exceptions.

194. FAIR, REV, BARTHOLOMEW FRANCIS, A.B., S.T.L., J.C.L., The Impediment of Abduction.

195. GALLAGHER, REV. THOMAS RAPHAEL, O.P., A.B., S.T.Lr., J.C.D., The Examination of the Qualities of the Ordinand, X-166 pp., 1944.

196. GANNON, REV. JOHN MARK, S.T.L., J.C.L., The Interstices Required for the Promotion to Orders, XII-100 pp., 1944.

197. GOLDSMITH, REV. J. WILLIAM, B.C.S. S.T.L., J.C.D., The Competence of Church and State over Marriage—Disputed Points, X-128 pp., 1944.

198. GOODWINE, REV. JOSEPH GERARD, A.B., S.T.B., J.C.D., The Reception of Converts, XIV-326 pp., 1944.

199. KOWALSKI, REV. ROMUALD EUGENE, O.F.M., A.B., J.C.D., Sustenance of Religious Houses of Regulars, X-174 pp., 1944.

200. MCCOY, REV. ALAN EDWARD, O.F.M., J.C.D., Force and Fear in Relation to Delictual Imputability and Penal Responsibility, XII-160 pp., 1944.

201. MCDEVITT, REV. VINCENT JOHN, PH.B., S.T.L., J.C.L., Perjury.

202. MARTIN, REV. THOMAS OWEN, PH.D., S.T.D., J.C.D., Adverse Possession, Prescription and Limitation of Actions: The Canonical "Praescriptio," XX-208 pp., 1944.

203. MIKLOSOVIC, REV. PAUL JOHN, A.B., J.C.L., Attempted Marriages and Their Consequent Juridic Effects.

204. MUNDY, REV. THOMAS MAURICE, A.B., S.T.L., J.C.L., The Union of Parishes.

205. O'DEA, REV. JOHN COYLE, A.B., J.C.L., The Matrimonial Impediment of Nonage, VIII-136 pp., 1944.
206. OLALIA, REV. ALEXANDER AYSON, S.T.L., J.C.L., A Comparative Study of the Christian Constitution of States and the Constitution of the Philippine Commonwealth.
207. POISSON, REV. PIERRE-MARIE, C.S.C., A.B., PH.L., TH.L., J.C.L., Droits Patrimoniaux des Maisons et des Eglises Religieuses.
208. STADALNIKAS, REV. CASIMER JOSEPH, M.I.C., J.C.D., Reservation of Censures, X-141 pp., 1944.
209. SULLIVAN, REV. EUGENE HENRY, S.T.L., J.C.L., Proof of the Reception of the Sacraments.
210. VAUGHAN, REV. WILLIAM EDWARD, J.C.D., Constitutions for Diocesan Courts, X-210 pp., 1944.
211. PARO, REV. GINO, S.T.D., J.C.L., The Right of Apostolic Delegation.
212. BALZER, REV. RALPH FRANCIS, C.P., J.C.L., The Computation of Time in a Canonical Novitiate.
213. DOUGHERTY, REV. JOHN WHELAN, A.B., ST.L., J.C.L., De Inquisitione Speciali.
214. DZIOB, REV. MICHAEL WALTER, J.C.L., The Sacred Congregation for the Oriental Church.
215. EIDENSCHINK, REV. JOHN ALBERT, O.S.B., B.A., J.C.L., The Election of Bishops in the Letters of Pope Gregory the Great.
216. GILL, REV. NICHOLAS, C.P., J.C.L., The Spiritual Prefect in Clerical Religious Houses of Study.
217. HAYNES, REV. HARRY GERARD, S.T.L., J.C.L., The Privileges of Cardinals.
218. MCDEVITT, REV. GERALD VINCENT, S.T.L., J.C.L., The Renunciation of an Ecclesiastical Office.
219. MANNING, REV. JOSEPH LEROY, J.C.L., The Free Conferral of Offices.
220. MEYER, REV. LOUIS G., O.S.B., A.B., S.T.B., J.C.L., Alms-gathering by Religious.
221. O'DONNELL, REV. CLETUS FRANCIS, M.A., J.C.L., The Marriage of Minors.
222. PRUNSKIS, REV. JOSEPH, J.C.L., Comparative Law, Ecclesiastical and Civil, in Lithuanian Concordat.
223. SWEENEY, REV. FRANCIS PATRICK, C.SS.R., J.C.L., The Reduction of Clerics to the Lay State.
224. VOGELPOHL, REV. HENRY JOHN, J.C.L., The Simple Impediments to Holy Orders.

www.ingramcontent.com/pod-product-compliance
Lightning Source LLC
LaVergne TN
LVHW050203080826
844660LV00012B/344

* 9 7 8 0 8 1 3 2 2 4 0 3 9 *